LIVING BETWEEN WORLDS

BOOKS BY JAMES HOLLIS

Harold Pinter: The Poetics of Silence

The Middle Passage: From Misery to Meaning in Midlife

Under Saturn's Shadow: The Wounding and Healing of Men

Tracking the Gods: The Place of Myth in Modern Life

Swamplands of the Soul: New Life in Dismal Places

The Eden Project: In Search of the Magical Other

The Archetypal Imagination

Creating a Life: Finding Your Individual Path

On this Journey We Call Our Life: Living the Questions

Mythologems: Incarnations of the Invisible World

*Finding Meaning in the Second Half of Life:
How to Finally, Really Grow Up*

Why Good People Do Bad Things: Understanding Our Darker Selves

What Matters Most: Living a More Considered Life

Hauntings: Dispelling the Ghosts Who Run Our Lives

Living an Examined Life: Wisdom for the Second Half of the Journey

LIVING
BETWEEN
WORLDS

Finding Personal Resilience
in Changing Times

James Hollis, PhD

sounds true
BOULDER, COLORADO

Sounds True

Boulder, CO 80306

Sounds True is a trademark of Sounds True, Inc.

Published 2020

Cover design by Jennifer Miles

Book design by Meredith March

Printed in the United States of America

Library of Congress Cataloging-in-Publication Data

Names: Hollis, James, 1940- author.
Title: Living between worlds : finding personal resilience in changing times / James Hollis.
Description: Boulder, CO : Sounds True, 2020. | Includes bibliographical references and index.
Identifiers: LCCN 2019038945 (print) | LCCN 2019038946 (ebook) | ISBN 9781683645610 (hardback) | ISBN 9781683645627 (ebook)
Subjects: LCSH: Resilience (Personality trait) | Civilization, Modern—Psychological aspects. | Jungian psychology.
Classification: LCC BF698.35.R47 H65 2020 (print) | LCC BF698.35.R47 (ebook) | DDC 155.2/4—dc23
LC record available at https://lccn.loc.gov/2019038945
LC ebook record available at https://lccn.loc.gov/2019038946

10 9 8 7 6 5 4 3 2 1

My thanks go to loved ones—my Jill and our children,
Taryn and Timothy, Jonah and Seah.

I also offer my gratitude to my friend and agent, Liz
Harrison; to my skilled editor, Jennifer Y. Brown; and to
the people of the Jung Society of Washington, DC.

And for my abiding friends,
in the order in which I met them—
Kent, Carl, Stephen, Travis, Sean, Martin, and Lloyd.

CONTENTS

Preface xi

CHAPTER 1 When the Old Map Disappears 1

CHAPTER 2 Life in the Between 9

CHAPTER 3 What Is Depth Psychology, and Why Does It Matter? 21

CHAPTER 4 Three Essential Principles of Depth Psychology 37

CHAPTER 5 Antigone, Hamlet, and Prufrock: Case Studies in the Search for Personal Resilience 63

CHAPTER 6 What Is Healing? 83

CHAPTER 7 The Maiden with No Hands: A Psycho-Mythic Interlude on Gender 95

CHAPTER 8 Navigating Changing Times 101

CHAPTER 9 A Map to Meaning: What We Can Learn from Jung 117

Afterword: Homecoming 141

Notes 147

Bibliography 153

Index 155

About the Author 167

We look at the world once, in childhood.
The rest is memory.

LOUISE GLÜCK

You'll never be complete,
and that's the way it should be.
Inside you one vault after another opens endlessly.
Don't be ashamed to be a human being—be proud.

TOMAS TRANSTRÖMER

You have to strive every minute to get rid of the life
you have planned in order to have the life that is
waiting to be yours.

JOSEPH CAMPBELL

If we define religion as the state of being grasped by an infinite concern we must say: Man in our time has lost such infinite concern. And the resurgence of religion is nothing but a desperate and mostly futile attempt to regain what has been lost.

PAUL TILLICH

I'd won the world
but like a
forsaken explorer,
I'd lost
my map.

ANNE SEXTON

PREFACE

I t is no secret that we live in troubled times. People in most eras—and most geographic and spiritual locations—have also thought themselves living in troubled times, and for sure, most individuals come to troubles sooner or later in the course of their own lifetime. Frequently, what we expect from life, from others, from ourselves is not what we experience. Frequently, what once seemed to make sense, now seems inadequate; what we thought we could count on, now uncertain. I have observed this pattern in history, in the news of our own day, and in the consulting room. It seems important, therefore, to look at what happens to us on both a cultural and a personal front during these in-between times when our old maps have eroded—or disappeared altogether.

Accordingly, the chapters herein define *in-between times* further and detail how the insights and methods of depth psychology may help us along the way to a life of personal dignity and meaning. Other chapters explore the nature of healing and review some of the many insights from the founder of analytic psychology, Carl Jung. Still others examine guideposts left for us by folklore, the classics, and Western literature. Although I must employ one-dimensional sentences with a beginning, middle, and end, written in a linear sequence, these themes keep threading back and forth upon each other throughout the chapters because they are all part of our three-dimensional experience of the perplexities of being human. It is always a challenge to represent the globe with a paper map, but I shall do my best to offer what cartography skills I have gained over my lifetime.

Pop theologies and pop psychologies do not weather well, and the electronic toys we have to divert us will only bring us closer to a reckoning. In the 1840s, Danish theologian Søren Kierkegaard expressed his conviction that one may foresee the end of one's age but not save it. That is where I think we may be—not on the brink of the New Age but teetering at the edge of new barbarisms. It will take all the resolve and courage we can muster to hold to our values in the face of whatever emerges from our particular appointments with these liminal times. What are those values? Where do we find the means to persevere when all is being called into question?

Some good folks have disliked my books because they are too dark, don't talk very much about happiness, and never mention joy. To this I say, there are many books that do, and they often make promises they can't keep. If they did keep those promises, I would be in line right behind you. Happiness and joy are wonderful things, but they are always contextual, transitory; they cannot be forced by stint of will. I was joyful when my daughter Taryn was born, but it was a joy alloyed with worry for how she would fare in this world and whether I could protect her or even be a good enough father for her. I still worry about the same things for her, even though she is now more than a half-century old and taking care of herself quite well. I also experienced joy when the Eagles beat the Patriots in the Super Bowl, and that was, *ahem*, some seasons past—an eon ago it now seems.

Happiness and joy don't need to have books talk about them; they will take care of themselves without our futzing around. Happiness is a by-product of being in right relationship with our souls at any given moment. It can come in a variety of venues, but it cannot be willed into being. I would rather talk about the reality of our daily lives; the weight of history, both personal and political, that seems forever with us; and how hard it is to live an honest, decent, and authentic life, as I do believe we must so endeavor.

Neither will this book have a lot of "Tom and Sally" stories designed to disguise the tough stuff. I will cite real examples from real people when we might discern something from their lives that will help us in ours. If, however, you do not like how your life is turning out, you may need to see what "ideas" your life is serving, assess whether they are conscious or unconscious, and then try to get better ideas. To that end, I will talk about the cryptic, even unconscious, notions that we serve on a daily basis—the universal themes, motifs, and hidden agendas that are running our lives. Getting some idea about these "ideas" is the only way we can begin to challenge them and regain our soul's journey.

We are all in this together. I have learned so much from you, and I hope you can profit from some of the ideas of this book. All we can do here is our best to draft our own maps and try to help each other from time to time.

JAMES HOLLIS
Washington, DC
2019

1

When the Old Map Disappears

When men beheld swift deities descend,
Before the race was left alone with Time,
Homesick on Earth, and homeless to the end;
Before great Pan was dead.

EDWIN MARKHAM, "A Lyric of the Dawn"

Every transformation demands as its
precondition "the ending of a world"—the
collapse of an old philosophy of life.

C. G. Jung

More than two millennia ago, a terrifying rumor swept the Mediterranean cultures and caused panic. The rumor? The god Pan had died!

While I realize that this death escaped your notice and has not yet alarmed you, I can assure you that his passing has played a large role in your life. The loss of his vibrant energy plays no small part in the ills of the present day. But Pan is not the only "mortal god"—an oxymoron if ever there was one. Frequently, in the tides of human affairs, what we call "history," and in the tides of personal life, what we call "crisis," the dominant values, the prevailing energies, and the central metaphors decline and lose their energy. Something dies out, runs its course. Turgid and top heavy, it topples over, seeking replacement by something else. Then comes a very difficult in-between. What we thought we knew, what we thought we understood, what we thought was a reliable map of our world, all seem now to fail us.

Pan once floated our ships, set our courses, lit our fires; he was sexuality, pervasive desire, the very vegetal nature of our being that seeks expression through all of us, the denial of which has led to illness, neurosis, and the necessary invention of palliative psychotherapy and pharmacology. Given that nature and our egos abhor vacuums, Pan's absence was quickly replaced by theology, morality, and imposing institutions. However noble their intent, these surrogate gods have severely wounded us, separating us from our natural drives and instinctual promptings. As Jung noted, in the end, all of our problems stem from one source—that we are separated from our instincts. As Friedrich Nietzsche added, we are "the sick animal." Our surrogate gods have failed us, and the new ones have not yet arisen. We are once again between worlds.

In my forty years of psychoanalytic practice, I find this underlying pattern common to clients from all walks of life, with divergent presentational symptoms and life stories. Something is spent within them—something finished, played out, exhausted, even dead. Something "not yet" remains over the horizon, still unseen, perhaps not even there.

How many of us have done what we were "supposed to do"? And how well did that work out for us? Although we might have gained parental approval, promotion at work, approval from our self-selecting coterie, what wakes us at three in the morning, stands at the foot of the bed, and terrifies us? What produces those disturbing dreams? Why, having done the "right things," do we feel bored, listless, depressed even, utterly without spark or animation of the soul? How many of us have then made foolish choices, seeking desperately to reanimate our lives, driven, as Matthew Arnold expressed it in his poem "The Buried Life," by a "thirst to spend our fire and restless force"?[1]

As I reflect on this in-between state, an old and familiar pattern emerges. Identifying it has helped me be better present to people's sufferings, struggles, and aspirations. This pattern has so often been called a *passage*. In all passages, something is exhausted, something is lost and irretrievable, and something to replace it is not apparent. In all passages, there is a death of something—naiveté, the old road map, a plan, an expectation, a strategy, a story, and so on. And what is to come is not yet present, not available, at least not conscious. Sometimes those passages are abrupt and the in-between state short; sometimes this most difficult in-between takes years to play out. There is one clear consistency, however: nature, our nature, evolves by way of death. How else can something within us grow and emerge without clearing away the old? And that same nature is always seeking the next stage in service to its purposes—though certainly not to our comfort or control.

For those who stick it out, however, something larger is always wishing expression through them. I begin to appreciate the wisdom of Rainer Maria Rilke's observation that "our task is to be defeated by ever-larger things."[2] If I am overthrown by something larger than my ego, I am in a developmental versus a static process; I am called to grow despite my preference for ease, predictability, and control. Most of us, when we reflect on it, grow most out of our traumas, our disappointments, our defeats. Yes, we can pile those experiences on top of our troubled self-image and use them to flagellate ourselves, to stay mired in old and familiar places. Alternatively, we can move through—perhaps even beyond—them and toward the life that wants to live through us, rather than the one we planned.

If I am overthrown by something larger than my ego, I am called to grow despite my preference for ease, predictability, and control.

Again, Rilke, in his *Letters to a Young Poet*, speaks movingly of the ambivalence we all feel in those hours of uncertainty, of dark nights of the soul:

> So you must not be frightened if a sadness rises up before you, larger than any you have ever seen; if a restiveness, like light and cloud shadows, passes

over your hands and over all you do. You must think
that something is happening with you, that life has
not forgotten you, that it holds you in its hand; it
will not let you fall. Why do you want to shut out of
your life any uneasiness, any miseries, or any
depressions? For after all, you do not know what
work these conditions are doing inside you.[3]

DÉJÀ VU ALL OVER AGAIN

Nature neither cares for our comfort nor asks our opinion—although
it does seem interested in rapid recycling. We can observe this pattern
of emergence, fruition, exhaustion, decay, and decline in history everywhere, including in our own history. The dynamics of nature—the
birth/growth/death cycle—show up in each of our lives as well. Many
sensitive observers in the nineteenth century felt the slippage of firm
theological, metaphysical, moral ground from beneath their feet. Novelist George Eliot, after having translated *Das Leben Jesu*, a work of
modern critical scholarship that undermined traditional understandings and grounds for belief, was reported to have observed of the three
sources of inspiration in the past—God, Immortality, and Duty—that
the first two were no longer believable, but the third remained still
compelling. What a classic Victorian snare that was—to have lost, or
discarded, the metaphysical grounds for a belief and to yet remain
bound to the rules, expectations, and constrictions of the old ideas.
What a double bind! What a mess!

And then Nietzsche, over in Basel, pronounced the obituary when,
in his 1882 *Die Fröliche Wissenshaft* (*The Joyful Science*), he wrote:

> God is dead. God remains dead. And we have killed
> him. How shall we comfort ourselves, the murderers
> of all murderers? What was holiest and mightiest of
> all that the world has yet owned has bled to death
> under our knives: who will wipe this blood off us?
> What water is there for us to clean ourselves? What

festivals of atonement, what sacred games shall we have to invent? Is not the greatness of this deed too great for us? Must we ourselves not become gods simply to appear worthy of it?[4]

Fyodor Dostoevsky, in the 1860s, predicted all this and noted that without God, all things are possible—all things. So, we have, as the children of these thoughtful ancestors, taken on the powers of the gods, split the atom, and loosed the genie. As a consequence, as William Butler Yeats so memorably noted in "Nineteen Hundred and Nineteen":

Now days are dragon-ridden, the nightmare
Rides upon sleep.[5]

OLD GODS WITH NEW NAMES

An intersection of historic movements and personal crisis occurred in my own life some decades ago. In the 1970s, in a class in Zurich, I heard this paragraph, written by Jung. It changed my life:

We think we can congratulate ourselves on having already reached such a pinnacle of clarity, imagining that we have left all these phantasmal gods far behind. But what we have left behind are only verbal specters, not the psychic facts that were responsible for the birth of the gods. We are still as much possessed by autonomous psychic contents as if they were Olympians. Today they are called phobias, obsessions, and so forth; in a word, neurotic symptoms. The gods have become diseases; Zeus no longer rules Olympus but rather the solar plexus, and produces curious specimens for the doctor's consulting room, or disorders the brains of politicians and journalists who unwillingly let loose psychic epidemics on the world.[6]

These words both shook me and helped me understand my own confusions. They ultimately helped me mediate—perhaps began the healing of—the split between my religious tradition and my emotional reality, a split that had caused me no little suffering and seemed irresolvable. Exploring the meaning of that paragraph by Jung led to my thesis at the Jung Institute and to the book *Tracking the Gods: The Place of Myth in Modern Life*. So, before exploring fully how this issue applies to all of us, let us unpack that seminal paragraph and the insights it can offer as we seek to replace our disintegrating maps.

First, we must acknowledge a tendency to think that *"Myth" is other people's religions, not mine—mine is the truth!* One of our closest beliefs is that our complex-driven "rationality" is capable of a discernment, a grasping of truth, denied to others. Therefore, in our primitivism, we are shielded from the irony that our historic condescension toward others' beliefs as myths will someday be seen with condescension by those who replace us.

Second, we must recognize that a "god" is encountered whenever we are engaged by the Wholly Other, the Other that is *transcendent* to our ego-complexed sense of reality. This is the *Primary Phenomenon*—that which appears to us as causal, a priori, not caused by anything else, inherently unknowable.

The ego, however, attaches to the *epiphenomenal*, or secondary, images, which arise out of such encounters with the Wholly Other rather than from the energy that phenomenologically gave rise to that image. Our ego state desires the predictable, the knowable, the manageable; it therefore grows bewitched by the image, rather than by the autonomous, invisible energy that infused that tangible image with numinosity. There was a time, for example, when the deity Zeus was charged with that luminous energy; but today, he is only a *concept*, moving neither heart nor mind. Still, our ego frame often remains bewitched by the literalism of confusing the name *Zeus* with the energy that once animated it.

Western and Eastern philosophy, as well as psychology and neurology, agree that we cannot know any phenomena directly; we can only know our *subjective* rendering of them. Hence, metaphysical theology—religion—is necessarily replaced by phenomenology, depth psychology, and their subjective descriptions of our internal experience.

This brings to mind a client who was wrestling with his spiritual understanding. He dreamt that he was in conversation with a group of people. He explained to them his realization that it was important to recognize that light was not the container but rather the energy that illumined that container. He felt a lot of pushback from the dream group about this assertion, but I told him that his unconscious had gotten it right. *Light is energy*, not a bulb. Bulbs burn out, but the energy renews and is ready to enter a new container for an uncertain length of time. His childhood concepts, imposed on him with perhaps the best of intentions, no longer carried the energy. He felt guilty that he could not embrace the old concepts, even though no one would keep old, burned-out bulbs around the house. And yet we do that all the time with old, burned-out concepts, exhausted understandings. The key then is to see where that energy has gone and begin to track where it is now.

So, the bright crew of Mount Olympus have not died; instead, they have been transplanted by the relocation of energies, though the husk of their presence remains. Given Jung's definition of a neurosis as *a neglected or repressed God*, we are still at the mercy of those energies that were once embodied in those Bright Presences atop Olympus. Rather than say we are possessed by Aphrodite or abandoned by her, we can purchase a self-help book on love's disorders and gain five easy steps for her retrieval. Rather than say we are in the grip of mad Ares, we feel inflamed by righteous anger and justify the right to strike our neighbor. And so on. We may believe we have left all those antique personages behind, but we remain gripped by the timeless energies they once personified. As Jung pointed out, our ancestors believed in gods; we believe in vitamins—both invisible.

As Jung pointed out, our ancestors believed in gods; we believe in vitamins—both invisible.

On the personal level, we suffer these displaced energies as neuroses. In an age of great material access, we suffer dislocations from the energies of our deepest being and, in return, suffer emptiness, anomie, aimlessness—all sicknesses of the soul. While most therapists address behaviors, thought processes, and biology, would it not make more sense to ask where the energy has relocated?

On a collective level, our culture's treatment plans for the absence of a personal, intimate relationship with the gods are materialism, hedonism, narcissism, and nationalism, as well as a coursing nostalgia for a world that never really existed. Our contemporary *Odysseys* are redirected to the Apple Store, the palliative pharmacy, or forays along the River Amazon Prime. Guided by Google, whereby all things are knowable, we wonder why we are so absent-spirited, so lost, and so adrift. We may say that these secular surrogates, these "isms," constitute our values, our de facto religions, those in which we most invest our energies. But we have to ask the obvious question, *How well are they working for us?* And to what zones transcendent do they link us? Is there a more effective, less damaging treatment plan for our malaise?

American poet Archibald MacLeish put it succinctly in his poem "Hypocrite Auteur":

> A world ends when its metaphor has died. . . .
> It perishes when those images, though seen,
> No longer mean.[7]

2

Life in the Between

Any uncertainty about the God-image causes a
profound uneasiness in the Self, for which reason
the question is generally ignored because of its
painfulness. But that does not mean it remains unasked
in the unconscious. What is more, it is answered by
views and beliefs like materialism, atheism, and similar
substitutes, which spread like epidemics.

C. G. Jung

So, then, where are we *today*? Something has ended! We are
between metaphors, those images that mobilize our resources,
that give us a sense of purpose, direction, and momentum. The
crises of our time are, for most parts of the world, not those that troubled and destroyed our ancestors. Despite the horrific bloodshed of
World Wars I and II, the great destructions of Famine, Plague, and
War have largely been contained in most parts of the world. They are
seen today as no longer driven by the gods but as manageable problems, *if* we are wise and disciplined in our approach to them.

In Dante's time, this life was generally perceived as but an ante-
chamber to the real life, allowing one to find courage to survive the
appalling conditions that were the lot of most humans. Rulers were
divinely appointed, so an attack on them was an attack on Divinity, a

dual crime. Today, most of us no longer believe we are we here to serve the monarch, or God's representatives on earth; rather, they are here to serve *us*, to make the conditions of life more congenial to our greatest fantasized goal: abiding *Happiness*! And if we do not much cotton to receiving our reward in the afterlife, then the modern State is saddled with the task. In addition to providing security, modern governments are tasked with providing conditions for the happiness of their citizens, and yet, as Aleksandr Solzhenitsyn wrote, "How long would it take to understand that the life of a community cannot be reduced to politics or wholly encompassed by government? Our age is a mere film on the surface of time."[1]

What is replacing the old order, the old gods, the old certainties? Well, for one thing, there is a profound cultural investment in our longevity, our health, and even the fantasy (perhaps, delusion) of sustaining life beyond the limits of nature. We have indeed already achieved marvelous improvements of our health and longevity. Life in the classical era was thought to last, as a statistical average, twenty some years. In the North America of 1900, it was forty-seven years. In the Western world today, it is nearing eighty, a stunning extension of life on this planet in a relatively short period. Even more, given the popular fantasy of the goal of life as happiness, surely we must also be able to live longer, to enjoy that happiness once reserved for the immortals alone. And so, *how happy are we?* As one character says to the other in Samuel Beckett's *Waiting for Godot*: "We are happy. . . . What do we do now, now that we are happy?"[2] (This must precede a very long pause in the dialogue, one in which the audience is getting restless.)

Now that we have achieved the contentment of the gods, whatever are we to do? We must do something, surely, and then do more of it. How do we fill our hours until the Guy with the Scythe arrives? Staying busy will surely hold off the anxiety, won't it?

We all know we have the comforts of shopping, the urgent distraction of connecting with the "other" that for some—for many, in fact—offers the momentary delusion of connection to something that matters. Just witness the feeding frenzy of Black Friday, gleefully filmed by television stations each holiday shopping season. The lusting faces right out of Hieronymus Bosch and Bruegel the Elder, the anticipation, the frenetic rush, the pushing aside of neighbors, the orgasmic bliss when one walks out holding a flat-screen television. If we were to flash forward a few weeks later, would we wonder how many found their melancholia comforted by that electronic object before them, or how many are still dealing with heartache, anxiety, and loss, despite acquiring, after long waits in line, the latest electronic gizmo? I am not criticizing these purchases, as I own some of these items myself. Rather, I empathize with the sad letdown that inevitably occurs when we ask more of the other, whether person or object, than the other can ever provide. What then? Whither to the soul?

In the seventeenth century, Blaise Pascal identified this phenomenon, noting that even the members of the French court, with all their privileges, grew weary, despondent, anxious when left alone with their own souls. So, *divertissement*, or diversion, has become a modern treatment plan for all that afflicts us when the diversion once again disappoints. But from what are we diverting, one asks? The answer varies from person to person, but it is safe to say that we seek distraction from the terrible longing the soul feels for connection with the mystery of being here.

The erosion of tribal images linking people to those mysteries is the great anguish of the modern world. We may think we have achieved progress, even sophistication, over our simpler ancestors, but the trade-off is the pervasive loss of a felt connection to that which feeds and sustains the soul. When ordinary distraction does not work to reestablish that connection, we have the thousand anodynes of chemical and ideological soporifics. This is not unique to our era; drugs and alcohol have been with us for millennia. When things get difficult, we get stoned, we drink until we feel no pain. Yet these efforts tend to awaken the same old pain while also generating new levels of discord. We also often turn to food as a treatment plan. Who does not project the need for the primal nurturant source onto food, the staff of life, the necessary daily bread? All addictions are anxiety management systems. They all "work" to a small degree; otherwise, we would not offer them as much committed energy as we do. And when none of these truly "work," there is always the referred anger, the sense of betrayal, of something stolen from us, which we call *righteous violence*. How energizing and distracting it is to be angry, to be full of blood lust. Sensation piles on sensation, creating a culture of violence in due proportion to the experience of the violence done to our souls. As Lady Macduff put it a few generations back in the story of brother Macbeth:

I am in this earthly world—where to do harm
Is often laudable, to do good sometime
Accounted dangerous folly.[3]

And when it is all too much to bear, too much to handle, we always have the comfort of a fatuous and sentimental return to the past. Such *nostalgia*, a word with an etymology that reveals its roots in pain and longing, shows up in the fantasy of thinking that the world of our ancestors, our parents, even our childhood was better. It wasn't, but it is comforting to think so. What we conveniently forget is that it wasn't all that great for women, for the poor, for minorities of all kinds, and it took a helluva a lot of denial and looking the other way to allow people to sustain that delusion. At its best, nostalgia is simply denial; at its worst, it is, "I've got mine, Jack. The hell with all the rest of you."

We may think we have achieved progress over our simpler ancestors, but the trade-off is the pervasive loss of a felt connection to that which feeds and sustains the soul.

We all have our own preferred fantasies. From childhood on, I placed my chips on education. I know it saved my life, and I have hoped it could save others. I have therefore devoted my childhood and my adult work life to education. If it helped me, I reasoned, it might rescue others as well. I am deeply grateful for the privileges that my education has brought me and the fine people with whom I have had the honor to learn from, teach, or mentor. And yet, it is easy to find evidence of our deplorable general level of education, our impoverished capacity to spot argumentative fallacies. The willingness to confess ignorance as the beginning of wisdom, the ability to sift and sort through the blizzard of information to discern what is most deeply true versus that which triggers our complexes and shallow desires for vindication—these are sadly missing in a public so easily swayed by distractions, fears, and showy whiz-bangs. We can see it in history's theater, in the *panem et circum*, the bread and circuses that the emperors once used to distract their people from the opportunistic wars, the predatory seizure of the common good, the privileging of the few to the plight of the many. We suffer the same dismal phenomena in our popular, social, and political cultures. Today, the online arena is far more sophisticated, diverting, and entertaining than even watching the lions devour the minority du jour in the coliseums of antiquity.

FUNDAMENTALISM AND SCIENTISM: THE NEW MYTHOLOGIES

If the self-deception of nostalgia for a mythical past is unsatisfactory and if education has eroded, what guiding images help frame our experience, give us a direction, a context, and a set of reciprocal expectations? How can we live in this great *in-between* that comes to all civilizations and to each of us individually from time to time?

In the civilizations proceeding us, most people believed there was a cosmic plan, an enfolding and unfolding energy of which they were a part. If a sparrow fell, it was part of God's plan, as were death, disease, and famine. While humans might have had an attitude about that, they did not often question the implacability of those forces, nor did they question their own ultimate vindication and restoration in a plane far beyond this. The key was to live in accord with the will of the gods as best as one could figure that out: don't espouse that thought, don't cross this line, be humble and trust. Today, if a child dies of disease, we expect the Centers for Disease Control to exercise vigilance in apprehending which viral visitant has encroached into *our* world and to then plan a repellent. If a plane falls from the sky, we expect the National Transportation Safety Board to figure out why and to correct the problem before *my* plane takes off. This shift of expectation, this locus of problem solving, depends not only on the marvelous achievements of science and technology over the past centuries but also often on a naive trust in science called "scientism." As a new myth, scientism is afforded huge latitude of trust and investment, with very little thought for consequences or for how we are to respond to the summons to grow up and live with an essential and personal powerlessness before an inexplicable mystery.

At the other psychological extreme is rabid fundamentalism, as fixed in ferocity as it is threatened by ambiguity, uncertainty, and powerlessness. As much as we claim to value education, forty-six percent, or nearly half, of the American people, despite massive evidence to the contrary, believe that "God" created humans in their present form within the past several thousand years. Despite the preponderance of fossil, animal, and archaeological evidence, many still cherish the thought that we are both the most recent arrivals and clearly, of course, the apex of all this history at the same time. Many defend creationism with fervor, even though it is full of gaps and contradictions that no reasonable, thoughtful investigator would even consider. Nearly half of Americans embrace this know-nothingism, and why? The answer is articulated best by Jung: it is a response born of pathogenic *complexes*, especially those driven by the anxiety generated by ambiguity and uncertainty. It is far scarier to think of the universe as driven by algorithms and impersonal forces than to project an authoritarian, parental personality onto the vast, expanding cosmos, to believe that *Someone* is in charge and purposefully unfolding history to our benefit. It speaks to our insecurity, our infantilism, that so many of us are willing to accept the most puerile of fantasies as a treatment plan rather than to grow up and confront the universe as essentially implacably Other and forever unknowable.

> It is far scarier to think of the universe as driven by algorithms and impersonal forces than to believe that *Someone* is in charge.

It is worth noting, however, that scientific "certainties" can still appeal to a fundamentalist. Although their physics, archaeology, and geology are limited to the past six thousand years, even the most devout creationist today will not walk into an emergency room and insist that he or she be given "only the treatment available to Moses, or Jesus, or Mohammed, and of course, don't bother with that anesthetic stuff. And, while I am here, why not trepan my brain and let those evil spirits out?"

Assuredly, our minds and our methods have produced wondrous accomplishments over the past few centuries; however, there is a Faustian pact here. It is a strange paradox, a revised de facto contract that Yuval Noah Harari notes in his *Homo Deus: A Brief History of Tomorrow*: "Humans agree to give up *meaning* in exchange for *power*."[4] In other words, we are presumably no longer actors in some cosmic script but the uncertain engineers of our own fates. In this postmodern myth, there is no cosmic script, no happy ending, nothing to give meaning. As Harari continues, "If modernity has a motto, it is 'shit happens.'" And it is all up to us to fix it.

The *Imago Dei*, or god-image, varies from age to age. Consider an example: For a short while at the end of the eighteenth and well into the nineteenth century, the god-image was the "Machine," which is why we have neuroses rather than something else. The word *neurosis* arose in Scotland in the 1790s, amid the emergence of the machine age, when a physician named William Cullen speculated that our emotional disturbances derive from flaws or impediments in the neurological "machine" that we are. To understand that machine is to find how to fix the flaws. Later, other emerging metaphors replaced this image. In the late twentieth century, for example, American psychologist James Hillman saw the battle of the gods decided in favor of the great god "Economics." More people's lives, values, choices, and energies offered service to this demanding god than to any other value. As a treatment plan for the vast absences in our spiritual life, the modernist treatment plan is especially driven by the stepchild of the god Economics, named "Materialism." When life gets difficult, go shopping. Until they were replaced by the ease of internet shopping, vast, brightly lit malls were temples drawing the faithful.

Ominously, Harari identifies the currently shifting, emergent god-term "Data," or perhaps "Big Data." Those who mine your spending habits, your social media choices, your Google choices have accumulated, in a short time, an emotional, spiritual, economic, political, and cultural profile of you. As this file accumulates, they "know" you better than your parents, even your partners, know you. Recently, a board member of the Jung Society of Washington, DC, reported visiting a branch store of a national chain. She talked to no one, never used her credit card, never made a purchase; she did nothing other than look and walk out. Three days later, she got a postcard thanking her for her visit. Did they read her credit card electronically? Employ facial recognition? Track her cell phone? What? And who sold that information to the marketers? Harari makes the compelling claim that Data is the new god, not only appearing in the machines that monitor us constantly but also "reading" our lifestyle choices, exercising sophisticated stratagems to manipulate our values and choices, exercising as much influence over our lives as the unconscious itself. The Russian government's proven interference in the U.S. electoral process is a notable example of such manipulation. The movement of our culture to one driven by artificial intelligence (A.I.) is producing what science fiction writer Vernor Vinge in 1993 called "the Singularity," his term for a moment in cultural history when the outmoded models of behavior and understanding are replaced by insurgent others at a pace beyond human comprehension and control.[5] This moment is not "out there" but already upon us, just as global warming is not a theory but a palpable reality. In this paradigm shift, A.I. proves to be more agile, faster, and more capable than human intelligence. The implications of this current in-between time are already upon us and exercising more influence in our lives than we know. It is not paranoia to surmise, however, that someone else does know and is paying attention.

HISTORIC RESPONSES TO TIMES OF CHANGE

How then can one find one's way in this world without a stable map, a reliable set of constructs, and tons of communal support? This is precisely the dilemma that the young Jung found in his culture, in his family of origin, and in himself as he approached adulthood. When he asked his cleric father probing questions about why his father believed what he professed, Jung got "only believe" in return. When Jung turned to his emotionally unstable mother, he got a séance, a magic channel to the "beyond." Away from home and out in the world, he would say, "When I think of *Father*, I think of *powerlessness*; when I think of *Mother*, I think of *unreliable*." How far through this forest of choices and values, which we all face, could anyone get with powerlessness and unreliability as the anchors of their personal structure? No wonder Jung sought another path.

Over time, Jung concluded that there was within each of us a deep resilience guided by some locus of knowing, independent of ego consciousness; a center that produces our dreams to correct us, symptoms to challenge us, and visions to inspire us. His was not an amateur's trust in impulse or a captivation by psychological complex; it was a long, patient, humbling attendance upon the *psyche*, or *soul*, and its perspicacious permutations.

Within each of us is a deep resilience guided by some *locus of knowing*, independent of ego consciousness.

All of Jung's intense exploration occurred in the context of cultural ferment and dislocation. While he was most intensely engaged in an investigation of the inner terrain of the human soul, most of Europe was engaged in a vast bloodletting, the consequences of which we are still suffering a century later. One of those consequences was a still more destructive war that followed. In a 1939 speech in London, Jung noted how, absent a sense of connection to something numinous, we even create disturbances:

> [People] are simply sick of the whole thing, sick of that banal life, and therefore they *want* sensation. . . . They are all *glad* when there is a war: they say, "Thank heaven, now something is going to happen—*something bigger than ourselves*." (emphasis added)[6]

In his novel *The Fall*, Albert Camus notes how excited and pleased everyone in the neighborhood is when there is a salacious scandal, especially if attached to a murder. It lifts everyone out of the deadly, ennui-producing routinization of life that deadens the soul. Violence appeals because it shatters the constrictive, predictive deadness of normality. Jung's last sentence—"something bigger than ourselves"—reveals our hunger for more than the ego-bound world. Beneath it all, Jung goes on to say in his speech, is "a terrific fear of loneliness."

Reportedly, our ancestors lived in a moment when the images of their tribe still linked them in felt ways to the transcendent Other—be it cosmos and its gods, to both generative and devouring nature, to tribal belonging and matrix, or to self and its great uncertainties. As we all know, those affectively charged links have eroded and thrown people back either upon themselves or upon the social palliatives their age has produced. So, if we lack a sense of our own soul and its daily journey, we may preoccupy ourselves with the lives of various strangers, even some called celebrities—those who may not have accomplished anything of note (and I quickly think of many examples) but are simply known for being known. Our ubiquitous treatment plan for disconnection is "distraction," the latest news ("if it bleeds, it leads"), the current scandal, or the imminent threat from some vector. Additionally, we have a pharmaceutical industry churning out meds for diseases not even described yet in the off chance that off-label uses for the new compounds may be found and, with that, an economic bonanza.

When Nietzsche proclaimed the death of God, he was making neither a theological nor a metaphysical assertion. He was speaking psychologically, for he simply looked around, watched his neighbors, and perceived the religious of his time as dispirited, formulaic, cautious, timid-souled, and lacking in energy. He felt, for example, that a religion like Christianity would only survive if it returned to the Jesus as the ecstatic god of the grape. He could only worship a "dancing god." He valorized the role of energizing our spirit when the soul is meaningfully engaged. But what happens when it is not?

In 1958, an age of general conformism and banality (I know because I was there), theologian Paul Tillich wrote an essay titled "The Lost Dimension in Religion," published in *The Saturday Evening Post*. In it, he observed,

It means that man has lost an answer to the question: What is the meaning of life? Where do we come from, where do we go to? What shall we do, what should we become in the short stretch between birth and death? Such questions are not answered or even asked if the "dimension of depth" is lost. And this is precisely what has happened to man in our period of history. He has lost the courage to ask such questions with an infinite seriousness—as former generations did—and he has lost the courage to receive answers to these questions, wherever they may come from.[7]

In this vast treatment plan for the disconnect that we feel from the larger energies of the universe, for all the cacophonous distractions of the hour, we all know something is missing, something aches in our souls, something longs for linkage to that which is larger.

So there it is. The gods have departed, left us to our own devices, and it's not going so well. We work assiduously at denial, convinced of our purblind assertions of certainty, partaking of a thousand distracting, numbing, addictive, seductive treatment plans that leave us so palpably alone, so lonely, and so terribly full of longing.

WHAT IS OUR CALLING IN TIMES IN-BETWEEN?

Over the past couple years, more than one person has asked me, "How can we continue to live in such a time as ours?" They feel violated by the abrogation of the social contract asking consideration, reciprocity, fair play, and civility of us and its replacement by cynicism, corruption, and degradation of values. The answer to them is simple, "How can we not?" All ages have their problems, and most of ours are First World problems. Most of us have grown to take food, shelter, and relative security for granted. Our life, in fact, is *much* easier than the lives of our ancestors, *much* easier, even, than Jung's life. We do well to look to those who weathered such rough seas. In times of cultural confusion, of paradigm shifts, of in-between times, and of personal crisis, the place to which we all must come is this:

- You are defined by what lies most deeply within, by your values, and by your actions.

- The acts of others, especially those who are disordered, do not define you.

- Whatever the prevailing myths of the time, civilization always depends on the good people doing what is necessary for the daily maintenance of their society.

So, we all have both personal and social service to do in the healing of our time. Children must be comforted; classes must be held. Hospitals must open their doors; police, direct traffic; teachers, teach; and so on. The world does depend on each of us showing up, as often as we can, as best as we can. The gift of depth psychology is that it may help us find our way to our own "locus of knowing" and give us a compass to chart our way.

3

What Is Depth Psychology, and Why Does It Matter?

Consciousness is not
matter dreaming. If all the stars were added
together they would still not know it's spring.

JACK GILBERT

Psychology, as we know it, did not exist in the nineteenth century. This fledgling discipline, born of suffering, first found an unsteady foothold in the acceptable "sciences" as the study of "mind." This focus on "mind" does not begin to account for so much that we now take for granted—the power of the unconscious, the role of complexes, archetypal shaping processes, and so forth—but it was a beginning.

Out of that shaky beginning rose a desperate need to prove itself worthy of inclusion in the academic, medical, and professional world. That deep need haunts psychology to this day and produces an unfortunate splitting, a privileging of empirical tests of value rather than the mythopoetic world in which we all actually live. While well intended, this shift to the material has so often narrowed and trivialized the human condition, so often concluded that the real is what one can observe and perhaps measure, neglecting the fact that we all swim in mystery and the inexplicable.

Jung noted that psychology developed so late in the nineteenth century and became the last of the social sciences because the regions it explores were once mediated by tribal myths and the great religions. In other words, if one wished to know what the right course of action was, the big picture, most humans existed in a field of received authorities—perhaps the village shaman or the institution that towered above them. If one suffered unplanned consequences of a personal or transpersonal nature, one need only consult the scriptures, the ancient stories, where it was all laid out before them. Modern depth psychology had to be invented, Jung noted, because those received authorities had progressively lost their power to connect individuals, or even the tribe, to the transpersonal energies. This transition of "authority" is still going on in our era and represents the greatest shift of power from the collective to the individual in human history, if the individual can bear it.

I have often suggested, with deliberate hyperbole, that the last time the Western world made sense to both king and commoner was around 1320. I choose that moment as the time of Dante's *Comedia*, a dramatized portrait of a knowable, predictable *Weltanschauung*; an eternal structure of values; and a road map of consequences that reverberate through history. The twin outer representations of those longitudes and latitudes of the soul were the castle and the cathedral, both claiming divine sanction and earthly sovereignty. But implacable forces—such as the migration from cultivation of the earth toward urban environments; the Black Death, which rendered the authoritative powers impotent; the rise of a mercantile and increasingly educated middle class—eroded those powers and gradually shifted away from the fantasy that the real life is beyond this life toward "this worldly" values. Lost in this shuffle are the abiding questions of *What happens to the human soul?* and *What now is available to help us find our way?* Let us consider what psychology has to offer as a map, where it fails us, and how depth psychology answers that failure.

WHAT IS DEEPEST WITHIN?

First, ask yourself this question: What word or concept central to both *psychology* and *psychiatry* is almost wholly missing from modern treatment modalities? Ironically, it is *psyche*, which is the formative metaphor for these words, if not these practices.

The preponderance of modern psychological and psychiatric practice splits the person into behaviors, thoughts, and body chemistry—all presumably observable and potentially measurable. While we are all of these things, we are also something more—much more. You would be offended if someone simply cataloged your behaviors, summarized your thought processes, read your medical chart, and then said they know the real you; you would protest that you are something more than the sum of those parts. *Psyche* is the Greek word for "soul" and reminds us that we are, finally, the animal that desires meaning and suffers its loss. Of course, we are a set of behavioral patterns; reflexive, unexamined thought processes; and biological drives. But to limit our approach to the merely observable features of life is a failure of nerve to take on the larger, nonquantifiable questions of meaning.

Depth psychology differs from other forms of the discipline in that it is an effort to approach the whole person, to undertake dialogue with the essential mystery we all embody. We cannot undertake this deepened conversation without engaging the unconscious, that mysterious realm in which so much is hidden to us yet from which so much keeps spilling into our world.

Depth psychology differs from other forms of the discipline in that it is an effort to approach the whole person.

The problem with the unconscious is that it is *unconscious*. We cannot address it directly, but we can track, engage, and interpret its manifestations in our behavioral patterns, our interfering, our affect-laden thoughts, as well as in the disorders of our soul that manifest in our bodies. Each of these venues is an aperture into the dynamics of an active psyche seeking its healing, suffering interferences, and correcting our diversions.

The problem with the unconscious is that it is *unconscious*.

Strange as it may seem, one gift of the psyche is psychopathology, which is when we are sufficiently split off from our souls that the psyche protests and summons us to accountability. Depth psychology recognizes that the presence of symptoms—the depression, the anxiety disorder, the self-medication—is a natural expression of the psyche, a commentary on how our life is going from the soul's perspective. While the natural desire of ego consciousness, as well as of ordinary treatment modalities, is to remove psychopathology as quickly as possible, depth psychology respects this invitation to dialogue with our own depths. Thus, we are summoned to ask other questions:

- Why has this symptom come to me?
- What does it want from me?
- What correctives to my course must I consider?

When we recall that the etymology of psychopathology is "the expression of the suffering of a soul," then we are obliged to consider the question of *meaning*. Having received a set of instructions from my family or my culture on how to live my life, on how to be "successful," I do my best to meet those expectations. But strangely, the fulfillment of those goals may leave me flat, listless, even depressed. That autonomous withdrawal of energy and approval from some part of my soul is a summons for me to go back to the drawing board and reconfigure my life, my goals, my assumptions—perhaps, even my "authorities," my "gods."

Depth psychology is an effort to dialogue with ourselves more deeply than ordinary ego consciousness and most treatment modalities plan to go. While I may find that the life, the choices, the values, and the risks that the soul asks of me are challenging, threatening to my security and predictability, the gift of taking that risk is an experience of meaning. Depth psychology understands that the goal of life is not happiness, which is only transiently possible anyhow, but meaning, which abides.

ATTENDING TO OUR OWN STORIES—AND REWRITING THEM

Depth psychology is especially informed by the examination of our formative experiences—those primal, internalized "stories" or interpretations that took us off course, framed our relations to others, and came to own our daily lives. To excavate them is not to dwell on the past but to realize in what ways the past is still active within us, creating patterns, dictating diversions, diminishing freedom of choice. As William Faulkner observed, the past is not dead; it is not even past. From childhood on, we begin "reading" the world in our need to adapt, fit in, get our needs met, avoid harm, manage anxiety. We make our uncertain way by asking:

- Who are you?

- Who am I?

- What is the traffic between us?

- How am I to deal with this world?

- Am I acceptable as I am, or do I have to twist and torque myself into some other shape to receive your love?

These framing experiences come to us as fate; we have no choice over our family of origin, our culture, the incidents of our biographies. But as we "read" these events and derive primitive, partial, prejudicial interpretations of these experiences, we tend to continue serving them until other experiences give a different, freeing message. So, the "reading" of our life patterns tells us much about the formative stories to which our lives have been in service, brings them to consciousness, and provides an opportunity for larger, better stories to enhance our journeys. If we change only the behavior and ignore its charged locus in our unconscious, the early "story" will only migrate into a new venue, a different relationship, a recurrent dilemma. These emotionally charged "stories" or "complexes" are splinter personalities, fractal scripts, and somatic presences. Until the core perception or idea that generates the undesirable behavior, the avoidance, the self-defeating compliance is identified, challenged, and worked with over time, the psyche stays stuck, the soul stagnates, and suffering persists.

THE ROLE TENDING OUR DREAMS PLAYS IN SELF-GOVERNANCE

In addition to tracking symptoms to their revealing core, depth psychology especially respects that mysterious, autonomous process we call dreams. An old German proverb says, "Dreams are froth," and yet nature does not waste energy. Several times each night, whether or not we pay attention, the psyche creates a dramatic, narrative reaction to what is happening in our lives and how it is viewed from a perspective larger than that of the ego. If we track these dramatized narratives over time and learn their language, we gain a vital source of wisdom not available to ordinary consciousness. If we knew that the timeless sagacity of nature was available to our troubled, sometimes beleaguered egos, would it not make sense to stop and pay attention once in a while? Over time, dialogue with the mysterious source that produces our dreams—the same source, by the way, of our protesting symptoms—shifts our focus from outer distraction to a deeper seat of authority. If we had access to a wise sage who knew us better than we know ourselves, was invested in our well-being and in our taking greater ownership of our journeys, would it not make sense to seek the advice of that sage? The Self that transcends ego-consciousness *is* that sage, and it offers us that locus of personal authority. Disconnected from it, we serve our complexes, wounds, and received cultural and familial messages instead of serving the intent of our soul. Working with our dreams allows all of us to look within, to see the center of gravity shift from our many adaptations to the outer world to begin to trust that something within each of us knows what is right for us. Learning to trust that sorting process, to value that dialogue, and to risk relying on an internalized sense of authority is what restores our journey to us, bringing us back to our own souls.

The first half of life is preoccupied with adaptation, fitting in, learning roles and expectations. These often necessary compromises with the world around us seem to offer protection, acceptance by others, and anxiety management. But over the years, they also become imprisoning structures, reflexive responses, conditioned compliances. Accordingly, in the second half of life, we are challenged to recover our personal authority. Regaining personal, rather than acquired, authority is difficult and becomes a continuing life's work, so powerful and repetitive are the received instructions and scripts. Personal authority requires sifting through the immense traffic that courses through our minds every moment. *Which voices are those from my culture? Which from my family of origin? Which from my soul?* And then we must mobilize courage to act upon what is true. While that sounds simple in the abstract, in practice, it is difficult because it requires us to move into less familiar regions of choice and consequence. Even when the old "authorities" are constrictive, they remain attractive because they are so often enhanced through repetition. Stepping into a larger frame through dreamwork helps us move into a more authentic life, from the ineluctable consequences of fate to the possibilities of destiny. Tilting that balance is the responsibility of consciousness and the gift of depth psychology.

PRACTICES OF DEPTH PSYCHOLOGY: JOURNALS, DREAMS, AND ACTIVE IMAGINATION

Undertaking a dialogue with our own depths brings greater purpose, dignity, gravitas, and meaning in this journey we call our life. It helps make it *our* life and not someone else's. It involves a measure of discipline, to be sure, to check in with our own souls and to pull out from the melee of our journey, the noisy distractions of our necessary duties, to ask, *What's going on here?*

My friend and colleague Marion Woodman used to ask people, before they began therapy with her, to agree to devote one full hour every day to writing in their journals, practicing active imagination, working with their dreams. Many people, she said, would respond, "But I don't have that kind of time. I can't cut that out of my schedule." To which she replied, respectfully, "Then you're not serious about this work. What could be more important than this kind of encounter with the magnitude of your own soul's journey?"

Every day, some time should be set aside—perhaps in the morning, perhaps at night—to formally address the workings of your psychic life. There is more than one way to do this. Journaling is important because you don't just sit down and write, "Dear Diary, this is what happened today." Instead, you ask,

- What got touched today?
- What generated a significant amount of energy?
- Where did that energy come from?
- What did today's experience touch in my history?
- What satellite issues might that have activated?

Perhaps you had some conflict with someone in the course of the day that continues to ripple for you. It's easy to dismiss it as something that happened "out there." But you can also pursue it a little bit and ask, *Where does this come from in my history?* You may find that it stirs resonant rings of influence, fear of conflict, or the difficulty of holding one's own in the presence of a large Other. Your journaling needs to ask:

- What was that about?

- Where did that activate some aspect of my history?

- What do I need to know about that?

- How do I need to bring the wherewithal of my adult capacity to it?

As you pay attention in your journal, recognize that you don't have to enter it every day but rather when something significant occurs. I have often found that when people are driving away from a session, their best thought on that session comes to them because their material has been activated. Or they wake up with an insight at three o'clock the next morning. I always say to pay attention to those waking thoughts; write them down. Some of them are tied to our specific daily anxieties, yes, but many of them reveal things that have been triggered. We need to figure out what things have been triggered and why.

We also, from time to time, need to take on the technique of active imagination. Jung developed this in a profound way. It's not meditation, and it's not guided imagery; those are other kinds of techniques. As the name suggests, *active imagination* is about activating the image. Let's say, for example, I have a dream in which I'm in a house. There's a sinister presence there. I think someone is trying to kill me or has hostility toward me, and I wake up in an anxious state. From the ego standpoint, the most natural thing for me to do is get out of that house, forget the dream, ignore it. But on the soul's journey, I have to ask myself, *Why has this dream come?* Dreams are not arbitrary. They're not planted in our brain by alien forces. They are natural by-products of our psyche seeking its own healing and development. That's the thing you need to remember. Dreams come to us as part of the psyche's natural process of healing itself for developing our journey.

To apply active imagination to this dream, I would find a quiet place, not interrupted by telephones ringing or noisy traffic outside, and reenter the psychic space of the dream, which is the last thing the ego would normally want to do. And yet, the dream is a product of my own nature. Why should I be estranged from my own nature? What I seek to do then is to go back into that dream and ask myself, *What is this presence, this sinister threat?* I might enter that room, that space, and approach that person to ask, *Who are you? Why are you here?*

The first couple times you try active imagination, you may feel nothing has happened because the ego is still clinging to its conventional sense of reality. It doesn't want to be in that room. You might tell yourself, *Oh, I'm just making this stuff up.* I have had those reactions myself. But as you practice, you will begin to realize you can slip more easily into a subjective experience of that setting and ask, *Why have you come? What is it you want from me?*

Out of this questioning often comes the revelation that this presence, this energy, may be some part of us that has split off, that is actively angry toward us, or that is seeking our love, our healing, our reenergization. Or it allows us to recognize that perhaps there are certain forces in our environment that are dangerous and that require our attention.

From the standpoint of street logic, our outer sense of reality thinks, *Oh, what nonsense is this? You're just making up talk in your head.* But here's the thing to remember: much of our psychic life is unconscious; it only becomes conscious when it activates itself through or is embodied through an image such as a dream image or a behavioral pattern. If you've actually activated the image, then in that moment, you make something of that invisible world visible. By activating the image, which is what is meant by *active imagination*, you thereby make it available to consciousness. You're not there to control it, as that would be quite contrary to working with the psyche.

This is why I'm not an advocate of so-called lucid dreaming, where people try to enter their dreams and change the endings. To my mind, that defeats the whole purpose of dreamwork. That is the ego reasserting its sovereignty rather than asking, *Why has the psyche spoken to me in this way? What does it wish to tell me? What is it I need to learn here?*

Where do I need to be humbled in order to learn? I see the whole notion of lucid dreaming as contrary to soliciting the wisdom of our nature. It's the ego seeking to control the soul one more time in one more subtle way.

Journaling, active imagination, and dreamwork are all forms of paying attention: listening to the psyche as it manifests and realizing that some intelligence is there that transcends ordinary ego intelligence. Something seeks to connect with us, something that represents, if you will, the wisdom of nature. This idea does not necessarily fit into the informed intelligence of our culture with which we must deal every day, but it is something that is larger than this time and place. It is willing, in some way, to risk its investment in us. How dare we, then, not undertake a journey to that which is seeking its expression through us? When we do this, it may be a humbling process, but I think it gives a profound sense of personal purpose, depth, and dignity to our journey that no amount of outer accomplishments or recognition by the world can ever equal; it gives that inner conviction that we are living our journey as honestly and as faithfully as we can. All of us, I believe, are invited to that journey and are always equipped by nature for it. And we can thank depth psychology, and specifically the work of Jung, for giving us some of these tools with which to address it. When we do, we will find that the wisdom of the ancients is once again present to each of us.

THE STUDY OF LITERATURE AS THE STUDY OF SELF

We carry all our history with us. Something that seems quite remote from present awareness may in fact be playing out within us and may produce a familiar pattern, though we may not recognize it at the time. The human psyche is like an analog computer: it is always doing a rapid data search in our cumulative experience to learn whatever it might in order to cope with the new moment. While each moment is unique in all of history, our experience sometimes helps us cope with it in adequate, adaptive ways; otherwise, we would be overwhelmed by the encounter with a radically new moment, a new reality, a new set of features, in any changing moment.

However, that same analogical use of history can impose a less adaptive, less conscious, and therefore less appropriate response to the invitation of the new circumstances before us. If, for example, a person has learned to fear strangers, that person will likely stay risk averse and live in a narrower circle of possibilities. Most of us make these constrictive choices in everything from food preferences to artistic interests to unexamined belief systems. When you recognize such responses, ask yourself:

- Where did that come from in me?
- Where have I been here before?
- What is this in service to me, inside of me?

It is not what you are doing but rather what that choice is in service to inside of you that makes the difference. For example, you may choose not to respond to an invitation to a party and rationalize your choice as an energy-saving decision, when in fact an old fear-based avoidance has won the day.

These elementary questions are hardly foolproof, however, because all of us are frequently self-deluding and can facilely rationalize any behavior, any motive, any pattern rather than risk examining how it arises and what it serves. Just as it is an ugly sight to see how either sausages or laws are made, it is also distasteful to see what primal impulses and fears drive our daily choices. Still, we have a desire to know, to look at things psychologically. Jung had some wise advice on how to continue that process after beginning the forensic analysis of the self.

Anyone who wants to know the human psyche will learn next to nothing from experimental psychology. He would be better advised to abandon exact science, put away his scholar's gown, bid farewell to his study, and wander with human heart through the world. There, in the horrors of prisons, lunatic asylums and hospitals, in drab suburban pubs, in brothels and gambling-hells, in the salons of the elegant, the Stock Exchanges, socialist meetings, churches, revivalist gatherings and ecstatic sects, through love and hate, through the experience of passion in every form in his own body, he would reap richer stores of knowledge than textbooks a foot thick could give him, and he will know how to doctor the sick with a real knowledge of the human soul.[1]

So, with Jung's blessing, we may profitably leave behind the dusty volumes of past authorities as we seek to live an honest journey.

I maintain, however, that we dare not forget the timeless portrayal of the great artists. Depth psychology is an attempt to discern and track the movement of the invisible energies that move the visible world. Just as Dante sought to discern "the love that moves the sun and stars," so we seek the invisible threads that shape the contours of our unfolding tapestry. Personally, as far as formal learning goes, as opposed to maturational life experience, I have always considered a deep, disciplined experience in reading literature a better preparation for working with the psyche than the study of psychological theory and practice, especially as that theory and practice is taught in most modern psychology departments. Behavioral and cognitive methods, as sometimes useful as they may prove, also trivialize the depth, the intricacies, the anfractuosities of the human soul. Limiting the scope of one's investigation to the observable is to suffer the delusion that what runs the world is observable.

I justify the serious and sustained study of literature as a better preparation for engaging the depth of the human soul with these seven reasons:

1. The serious study of literature provides us with an enhanced capacity to "read" the metaphoric nature of behaviors, patterns, and motives. To discern what our behaviors are in secret service to is the only way to begin to approach an understanding and rapprochement with them.

2. The serious study of literature helps us assemble our own psychic thesaurus, our storehouse of images that provide analogies,

promote amplification, and illustrate our common issues and dilemmas in a wider perspective. As we will see in chapter 5, try as he might, Hamlet can only be Hamlet in the end. However, through the power of Shakespeare's imaginative gift, we can learn more about Hamlet's dilemma and ours, be the freer for it, and live a broader portion of the spectrum of experience than the troubled prince at Elsinore could approach. Hamlet broadens our imagination, even as he is constricted to the text the author gave him. For us, what can be imagined can be approached.

3. The serious study of literature increases our capacity to see the archetypal nature of individual cases, unique stories, and particular dilemmas, as well as the formative work of the Collective Unconscious in shaping our behaviors and cultural patterns. The archetypes that rise from the deep ravines of the human psyche are not contents; they are fundamental, patterning energies. As we see the liniments of the emergent form, so we know that we are seeing an individual ego state subsumed into a larger current of energy. We recognize the death/rebirth, the *catabasis/anabasis*, the ascent/descent pattern, the scapegoat mechanism, the penumbra of the Shadow passing over the sunlit field, and so on. We are all time-bound creatures, speeding toward our own extinction, but each of us is also a creature of a timeless drama. What we have felt, desired, and suffered has all been experienced long before us and will continue as long as we persist on this imperiled planet. Riven by the rush of transience, we see that we are also timeless actors in a larger drama than we imagine.

4. The serious study of literature enables us to explore a much wider range of choices than ordinary ego consciousness—a veritable miner's circle of light in a huge cavern of possibilities. We can learn new attitudes, new behaviors, new latitudes of action from literary characters, even as we become more sophisticated in the presence of hidden motives and troubling choices; we can sometimes even learn why things often do not turn out so well.

5. The serious study of literature broadens and deepens the parameters of the human condition. We learn from great literature why things recur in our lives—the cultural tumults and revolving epochs. Having digested the cumulative message of human folly and wisdom, we may still be surprised at what happens in our lives, but we won't be shocked. Just as clients have said to me while bringing in a stunning dream, "You are not going to believe this dream, Doc," I know that I will believe it because even though every dream is unique to the dreamer, I will have seen a form of it before, many times before. (Among the many surprises awaiting me as I began my analytic training many decades ago was the first encounter of receiving several dreams from different people with very similar, if not the same, images and motifs. I am not suggesting they are responding to a common social event, but something does get constellated that triggers an image, motif, or process along a path that others have trod before and tread with us still.)

6. The serious study of literature will lead us to recognize what has been called "the fiction of case histories." *Fiction* does not mean "falsehood." Coming from the Latin *facere*, it means "construct," just as *factories* construct things, and *fabric* is something we make to wear. These constructions may point us toward the truth. The ultimate truth of any person's soul is forever inextricable, forever mysterious. We can never fully plumb the telluric regions of human motivation or resistance or the chthonic depths of the unconscious, just as Picasso observed that art is a lie that tells us the truth and Magritte reminded us that we are not looking at a painting of a pipe but an arrangement of pigments on a canvas meant to trick the eye and brain by writing on the canvas itself—"*Ceci n'est une pipe.*" The naive, literal vision of the ego, which is how we most often see the world, sees the painting and says it's a pipe. Magritte reminds us, by hitting us over the head with the explanation on the surface of the canvas, "This is not a pipe; it is a squiggle of pigment on a canvas. And by the way, pipes smell like pipes, and this smells like oil."

Every case history is a "fiction." We are not seeing the person; we are seeing a window, an aperture, an angle of sight toward the person. Similarly, Aristotle felt art tells us more than history. While history is the lie the victors agree upon, as Napoleon cynically observed, Aristotle noted that even the most factually accurate history is seen through the distorting lens of the personality, psychology, and culturally selective biases of the historian. Being able to understand that our understanding is another "fiction," thrice removed as it is, a partial construct revealing some dimensions and concealing others, is a form of respect for the unique mystery that each of us is. We are more likely to be open to a larger frame of self-awareness if we understand that we are viewing only through our own distorting lenses.

7. The serious study of literature broadens our imagination. The German word for imagination, *Einbildungskraft*, literally means the "power of creating a picture." And *Fortbildung*, translated as "continuing education," means the broadening and strengthening of the pictures we have available to us. We are limited in our understanding of the world just as we are limited in our spectrum of pictures. The wider the spectrum, the greater the number of pictures, and the more abundant our capacity to apprehend the incredibly imaginative dynamics of the human psyche, its range, its permutations, its stunning parade of personae from St. Francis to Marquis de Sade, from Medea to Sappho, from Oedipus to Odysseus to Faust to Emma Bovary to Raskolnikov to Anna Karenina—all of them illustrating some aspect of the variegated human soul.

You might rationally ask, after this justification of the importance of the artist's imaginative powers, why did I then leave my early teaching of literature and the philosophic traditions of cultures to study psychology? The answer is both simple and complex, as all important things are. After twenty-five years immersed in the humanities, I came to recognize the need to discern the source of these images that shape our culture, from whence this rich thesaurus of archetypes derives, and to what larger invisible drama they were in service. That preoccupation has occupied the second half of my life, and I know I could have discovered neither the power of depth psychology nor the tools to track the invisible energies without the preparation of the first half. After some further exploration of depth psychology in the next chapter, we will return to literature in chapter 5.

4

Three Essential Principles
of Depth Psychology

Over the past four decades of working in both a psychiatric hospital and a private practice, I have reached some conclusions about what is going on beneath what transpires on the surface of our lives. Perhaps I can best explain by presenting these three somewhat arcane principles of depth psychology and then go on to unpack them and give you examples.

I. It's not about what it's about.

II. What you see is a compensation for what you don't see.

III. All is metaphor.

Now, what does all that mean? I am glad you asked.

I. It's not about what it's about.
So, what, then, is it about? This opaque maxim is meant to urge us to inquire more deeply. Many modern psychology and self-help books treat the symptoms without asking from whence they come and why they are so resistant to treatment.

In most instances, our symptoms tell us how and in what way we are driven by the anxiety experienced by our protective systems. In other words, our symptoms arise from our efforts to protect ourselves from anxiety and thereby serve a worthy motive. But our protective mechanisms themselves cause estrangement from our natural being and accumulate consequences of their own. For example, many of us procrastinate rather than face something that triggers anxiety, but, as we all know, this strategy produces problems of another kind. I recall that years ago, the New Jersey Dental Association created a billboard campaign that said, "Ignore your teeth, and they'll go away!" So, ignoring our problems and the tasks to which they call us causes the problems to go away, right? We all know the answer to that question: procrastination accumulates consequences that pile up until the treatment plan becomes worse than the original dilemma.

Having recognized that our procrastination can produce cumulative consequences, the tools of behavior modification and cognitive therapy can clearly be useful, but what if it's not about what it's about? What if the underground pool of anxiety all of us carry persists and shows up in another venue? When we turn to self-medication to assuage that anxiety, we may temporarily feel less stressed, and yet the consequences often pile still higher. Through the years, I have had many patients say that their use of antidepressants didn't solve their problems, but they did seem to worry less about them. Well, I can understand and sympathize that worrying less about something feels better than perseverative worry, but the consequences pile higher and higher. Often, it seems, we have to hurt enough to be motivated to do something about it.

DEALING WITH STUCK PLACES

Through the years in workshops on different topics, when I would ask a group to reflect on their "stuck places" in their lives, no one, on any of four continents, ever asked, after the translation was understood, what a "stuck place" was, nor did they hesitate in writing or speaking about their particular examples. Stuck places, therefore, are a good illustration of the conundrum that "it's not about what it's about."

Since we can so readily identify a stuck place and since the word *stuck* implies a judgment against ourselves, why is it so difficult to get unstuck and move forward? Let us examine some examples of experiences that each of has suffered in different areas of our lives.

From time to time, we identify a stuck place—an issue, a behavior, or an avoidance—that persists in troubling our conscience and in accumulating consequences. Among the most common are the inability to lose weight, to drink less, to exercise more. Many times, a person will set off earnestly with a will to do exactly that. Will, after all, is a most useful mobilization of our executive function; it can produce wonders of development, marvels of achievement. But as we know, will often flags and fails, and the same old, same old reconstitutes itself.

So, what is going on, and what are we to do?

Let us imagine a horizontal line across the top of this page but down perhaps twenty percent from the top. Above that line is the sphere of conscious life—who we think we are, and what and why we think we are doing whatever it is we are doing at the moment. Below that horizontal line is the vast sea of the unconscious about which we can, by definition, say almost nothing. We intuit that the unconscious is there and playing a substantive role in the conduct of daily life because unexpected consequences keep showing up, often producing outcomes contrary to our best intentions.

The place where the conscious and the unconscious meet is an uneasy frontier with no definable boundaries. No wonder there is often bad blood between the two spheres of influence as guerilla parties cross the border in both directions and make raids on the unsuspecting. That meeting place of force and counterforce shows up in conscious life as symptoms, troubling behaviors, and self-treatment plans. Our resistance to addressing this contretemps is clear and problematic. As one client said to me, quoting his Alcoholics Anonymous (AA) group, "This isn't working for me, but I do it very well." So it is that we perpetuate **"This isn't working for me, but I do it very well."** our stuckness and its cumulative consequences because it does work well for us—or so we think, until we look at the consequences. How does this ever get resolved, or does it?

We often stay stuck because ego consciousness is so easily distracted or lulled by the shabbiest of excuses or seduced by the flimsiest of strategies. And the stuckness persists. Accordingly, the only way through these dilemmas is "through" them, which is precisely what our protective mechanisms are trying to protect us from experiencing. The question then always comes down to this: *What anxiety is my stuckness protecting me from?* For example, let us say that you wish to speak up more forcefully, more directly; you may be angry with yourself in the face of your meek complicity and the lost opportunities this strategy accumulates. And yet to speak out, to step forward into the contested zone, is to experience an unacceptable flush of archaic anxiety. I say *archaic* because it draws from earliest pools of anxiety that every child incurs. As children, we are all surrounded by giants; we are lacking in essential knowledge of what is going on and are utterly dependent, frightened, and seeking protection from others. Flash forward a few decades, and a metaphoric donkey stands on our tongues, protecting us from imminent risk and deepening our further estrangement from our values and legitimate agendas.

Or consider, for example, the desire to eat less. Food is seldom neutral to humans. While food is fuel for the tank for the next stage of the journey, humans tend to consider food as something more important than putting gasoline in their cars. Food is "matter," but it is matter imbued with the invisible ingredients that feed our bodies and our spirits. *Matter*, of course, derives from the Latin *Mater*, "Mother," the nurturant source, without which we would perish. No wonder food gets such energy-charged projections. But it is also that which comforts, offers constancy, is familiar, promises reassurance and reward. If it weren't for excess calories, clogged arteries, and decreasing satisfaction as we exhaust the emotional resources of food, it would be a link to the mysteries, to the inexpressible but compelling needs of nurturance. We might rightly feel that it is perilous to say "no" to such resources, and so we stay stuck in our relationship to food.

More than one person has said to me over the decades, "I won't let go of 'this' until the 'that' is there for me." Such a sentiment is understandable, but it ratifies the stuckness. The question remains: *What anxiety is my stuckness protecting me from?* But there is a corollary question that quickly emerges. Anxiety is free floating, amorphous, and often unfathomable, and yet, like fog, it can block our moving forward. The task then is to ask, *What specific fears lie hidden within that paralyzing anxiety?* Anxiety is hard to confront, but fears, being specific, can be confronted. In most cases, our fears will not arise if we get unstuck, but in those cases when the fear does in fact materialize, we can deal with it by being the adult who has grown up and is now capable of insight and resilience, who can manage what was daunting to the child. Accordingly, we now see that our resistant behaviors are "logical" based on the premise they serve: *I avoid an unacceptable experience of anxiety through this behavior, a behavior that creates its own gradually increasing problems.*

If we are ever going to make progress against these self-defeating behaviors, we have to make a real effort, a probing forensic investigation, into what the "stuck place" is really about—that is, how does being stuck help us avoid anxiety, and how can we find a way to deal with it?

All of our anxieties, the existential threats to our well-being, can be catalogued under the twin categories of overwhelmment and abandonment. We learn early that the world is big and we are not; we learn that we are powerless against so many forces "out there." That message of fundamental overwhelmment is overlearned in all of us and sabotages the fact that we are brought into life with the guiding instincts and growing powers of resilience, as well as the adaptability that helps us take on those powers.

Abandonment is a valid existential threat as well, for we truly could not survive if caretakers of some form did not support us. Yet the insufficiency of any circumstance—be it troubled persons fate has placed in our way, socioeconomic deprivation, or social categories such as gender, race, sexual orientation, and the like—is interpreted by the child as a statement about his or her inherent worth. As children, we all "read" the world to see what the message is: *Who are you? Who am I? How are we to relate? Is life trustworthy? Am I acceptable as I am? Do I have to twist myself into something else to win your support?* Thus, the fated insufficiency of the world that we receive defines us until we learn otherwise. My own mother was born into poverty and was classified in all her school documents as "indigent," a word she did not understand. She never felt worthy of anything at all—nothing, all her life, nothing. Even as a child, I remember wanting to achieve something in order to make her feel better about herself. But by the time I had arrived, the message was too deeply imprinted, and no surrogate achievement by others could shake her core sense of unworthiness.

So, in our forensic investigation of the "stuck places," we have to ask ourselves: *What anxiety will be generated here if I stop being stuck? Will I have to face something that feels overwhelming to me and step out into the world to take it on? Or will I have to walk the shaky plank of diminished self-esteem to show up as myself in this strange theatrical production I call my life?* If, *IF*, we can answer the question of what we will have to face, we usually find that fear is chimerical—daunting to the child but quite manageable to the adult. If what we fear does come to pass, we will likely find that we are adults who can survive and prevail; the wave crashes over us but recedes and leaves us standing.

When we examine those fears, we find they usually are very primitive in their message: *If I do this, feel this, express this, you will punish me, or I will lose your approval and affection, and I will perish.* Yet, seldom, if ever, are those fears going to materialize. They are the simulacra of archaic anxieties of childhood, the ghostly hauntings of our defenseless past. If they were to materialize, would we not find our adulthood sufficient purchase on a ground firm enough to weather even that? Most of all, what is the cost of continuing stasis and stuckness when our being wishes to grow and develop? What betrayal of the soul transpires when we collude with our debilitating fears? And who, besides us, will pay those debts of unlived life—our children, our partners, our colleagues, our society? Do we not see that the best thing we can do for others is really to bring our best, most nearly authentic selves to engage them?

THE SAFE HARBOR OF ADDICTIONS

In looking further at the concept that "it is not about what it is about," we may profitably examine this principle in the context of the ubiquity of addictions. We live in an anxiety-ridden, addiction-directed society. We all have addictive behaviors, and the more we deny them, the more they have their foothold in our souls and own us.

The word *addiction* has become an ugly word, conjuring up ugly images: a car veering into the left lane, a person lying in the street, a shattered life. But addictive behaviors may be found in all of us, a truth revealed when we reflect on two elements common to all addictions.

The first idea is that addictions are *reflexive anxiety management systems*. Each of those words is important.

Since no human is free of anxiety, we all have our habituated, reflexive means of coping with it, whether or not the disturbing behavior is conscious. For example, many years ago, I used to allow patients to smoke in the consulting room, thinking that they had enough stress in their lives without my adding to it. However, one couple, chain smokers each, lit one cigarette after another and in a one-hour session totaled twelve cigarettes; that is six apiece. I counted. The smoke and smell hung in the room for days. From then on, I changed my policy. And yet, if someone had asked them, "Did you smoke during the session?" both would have said, "Yes, I had a cigarette." In other words, their reflexive management of anxiety through smoking was so conditioned, so habituated, that neither thought about it and how systemic it had become in their lives.

Stop and think how you might reflexively "manage" anxiety, or better, how you are repetitively managed *by* anxiety. The inner logic of an addictive pattern is that we suffer an unacceptable level of distress and, through connection with some "other," feel a momentary lowering of the disturbing affect. If, while reading this paragraph, your room is filling slowly with water, and yet your attention is so focused on the content that you do not attend the event consciously, the psyche nonetheless takes note and seeks to lessen the disturbance. Through experiment and exploration, each of us solicits a behavior that lowers the water level, at least momentarily. The next time this happens, the more likely the earlier behavior will be repeated, whether consciously or not. Therein lies the addictive hook—*the experience of momentary surcease of distress by a reflexive management system.*

Connecting with the "other" serves to lower the distress occasioned by our existential isolation, vulnerability, and dependencies. For many folks, the "other" is a substance: food, alcohol, purchasable material objects, a warm body. For still others, it is found through distractive "connections" with electronic devices, the internet, ideologies, compulsive exercise, prayer, mantras, and the like. For most of us, a common addictive pattern lies so much at the heart of daily life that we seldom accord its role in our psychological economy—namely, *routine.*

Routinization is a means by which the familiar is imposed upon the uncertain. Notice how we get bent out of shape by the traffic jam at rush hour, when the paper arrives late, when our plotted schedule is interrupted. The magnitude of our suffering is disproportionate to the minor provocation and indicates the arousal of anxiety.

The second key element of addiction is that our daily conscious life is repeatedly invaded by *unbidden ideas*. While these "ideas" are mostly unconscious, they have the power to stir anxiety within us. When people cling to food, for example, they are in the grip of a powerful, existentially threatening idea—namely, *If I do not have this object in hand, this comfort, what will be there for me in the darkness of this journey?* When we make this thought conscious, it may appear a peculiar, even ridiculous displacement of emotion onto matter, but in the symbolic world of the unconscious, our psyche moves us to fasten onto an object with its implied nurturant, its protective hope, as a stay against the anxiety in which we daily swim.

None of what we are discussing here is new—the record of addiction is as old as the human story. We find a notable and compelling portrait of a modern neurotic person like us in Shakespeare. The last thing we need to do is judge or shame any person for being human, for falling prey to "the thousand natural shocks that flesh is heir to," as brother Hamlet put it four centuries ago.[1] He is the same one who observed that he could be bounded in a walnut shell and count himself a king of infinite space did he not have bad dreams. He also illustrates the "Hamlet complex" that we all have—namely, there are things we know we should do, like give up an addiction, but for reasons we do not know, we do not or cannot.

One reason it is so difficult to break addictive patterns is that we are treating the reflexive behavior rather than the "idea" it was formed to treat.

Each New Year, we set off valiantly to address the problems of which we are so keenly aware, and yet we so often fail in our resolve. One reason it is so difficult to break addictive patterns is that we are treating the reflexive behavior rather than the "idea" it was formed to treat. Since our management systems wrap themselves around our core anxieties—fear of loss of autonomy, fear of the magnitude of our journey, fear of abandonment, and the like—we never get to the real issue. If we are ever to address an addiction, we have to finally address the unbidden ideas to which our psyches, and therefore our addictive strategies, are in service. These ideas are not shameful, although the consequences of some of our management systems often produce shaming consequences for us and for those around us.

The usual treatment plan for any addiction is to summon a heroic will. The heroic will is certainly a great asset, and few of us would accomplish anything in life without it. But the heroic will is often trumped by the depth, ubiquity, and energy of those intrusive ideas that spark addictive behavior. Thus, most of us fail to change our diet sufficiently over time because our will is subverted by an inner urgency. Or we fail to begin what we believe we should do or fail to stop doing what has proved detrimental to ourselves or others. Clearly, heroic will can only make certain headway for us, which is why dieting centers and fad diets are so profitable for the owners and why Twelve Step groups are so ubiquitous. (By the way, I am very much in support of Twelve Step programs, as they have proved more efficacious than most alternatives through the past eighty plus years.)

If ever we are to triumph over an addiction, we must first be summoned *to feel more consciously what we have already been feeling*, suffer what seems insufferable, and live through this experience without the reflexive management system. We never "solve" those unbidden ideas because they are an intimate part of our common human condition. We are born into perilous states, and we end by dying—so, have a nice day! The questions remain, however: To what degree is our life governed by these fears, and to what degree do our management systems own us or manage us, and with what troubling consequences?

How many of us are able to bring the core fears and anxieties into consciousness, to see and acknowledge what they are truly about? How many of us are able to go through those fears without the treatment plan we cobbled together?

Not only do addictions bring harmful consequences to our lives, they also narrow our lives as we get obsessional about our obsessional treatment plans for our obsessions. "Unbidden ideas" are obsessions, for they impose themselves upon us and cause distress. They are compulsions because we are driven to behaviors dedicated to their prospective amelioration. But our thoughts, behaviors, and lives get oriented around these intrusive ideas and are therefore narrowed. As Jungian analyst Marion Woodman once said, "Compulsions narrow life down until there is no living—existence perhaps, but no living."[2] In Greek mythology, Ixion is tied to a wheel that turns continuously in the underworld. Addictions oblige us to venture into our personal underworld wherein we experience the same thing over and over again, or, as noted by Satan in Paradise Lost, "Which way I fly is Hell; myself am Hell."[3] As Gregory Bateson has observed, obsessional drinkers believe they can challenge the "spirits." But the game is on, and more often the "spirits" win, so the drinkers are imprisoned by that which they first sought.

This hidden spiritual desire, this need for transcendent "connection," for "getting high," was identified in a letter exchange between Carl Jung and Bill W., who founded AA. Jung suggested to Bill that Twelve Step programs acknowledge the profound role of our spiritual hunger, our spiritual thirst. Unless the person can differentiate that quite legitimate, necessary motive from the substance upon which he or she has projected, that person will remain its bewitched captive.

Freeing ourselves from our addictive behaviors requires identifying what emotional reality or perception we are defending against through the addiction and risk bearing what has been perceived as unbearable. Going *through* the fear, rather than defending against it, is the only way we can stop Ixion's wheel. It is no shame to fear abandonment, suffer boredom, or experience depression. Until we can feel these things—really feel them and not anesthetize them—we will remain unmotivated to change our lives.

It is necessary to pierce the veil, deconstruct the mechanics of the addictive cycle, identify the primal, unassimilated idea for which our behaviors are a failing treatment plan. Then, as free persons, adults, we find we can in fact bear the unbearable, think the unthinkable, suffer the insufferable, and be free.

The key to identifying what it is about when it's not about what it's about, therefore, is to track the underground stream of anxiety. Yes, that sounds terribly reductive, but again, most of our behaviors are anxiety driven, as we realize once we really track them to their sources rather than simply rationalize away their noisome autonomy in our lives. That anxiety-generated system does not make us neurotic, enemies of ourselves—life is lethal, and real dangers do exist. What causes that inner splitting we call "neurosis" is when we ally against our nature as it seeks its legitimate expression in the world and instead identify with our treatment plans, our management systems. Whether those treatment plans involve avoidances, compliances, hypercontrol, addictions, distractions, or numbing, we remain self-defeating and estranged. This internal estrangement is only overcome by insight, courage, and persistence. Insight sometimes is the easy part. Courage is quite difficult to engage because our treatment plan is protecting us, and relinquishing those protections threatens our carefully negotiated rapprochement with life. Persistence is a function of character—whether we have the will, the commitment, the discipline to adhere to a disquieting path and to return to it when we stray. But figuring out what it is about when it is not about what it is about is the important first step, without which we stay stuck and at odds with ourselves.

In this way, we might revise our view that addictions are shameful and recognize that they are a rational response to a real anxiety. But in simply putting all that burden for resolution on the ego, we learn that we really have to ask what purpose the addiction serves and from what it is protecting us. When we consider what difficulties will occur when we do not activate the defense system, we realize the extraordinary power of the anxieties that sustain addictions. If what we discover can be confronted, then we may step into a larger journey, having discovered that it is not about what it is about.

II. What you see is a compensation for what you don't see.

The human psyche, differentiated as mind, body, spirit, and soul, is a self-regulating system. You are not governing your parasympathetic nervous system right now, but some agency within you clearly is. We all forget the wonder of this self-regulating system, take it for granted, and abuse it. Something in us always knows what is right for us and is undertaking measures to bring that confluence of will and nature about, even as it may be oppressed by the burdens and incursions of the outer world or opposed by our behaviors and treatment plans. The psyche is also compensatory: in daily life, complex-driven choices move us to one side or the other, while other energies seek to bring us back in line, back to our centering systems.

So, in looking at the principle that what we see is a compensation for what we don't see, let us recognize that what we see is the "treatment plan." What we don't see are the underlying forces that inform our every choice—those primary, anxiety-producing threats of overwhelmment and abandonment. The field of relationships illustrates this principle well. We claim to prize our relationships to others so highly; however, despite how much we value them, so many relationships are broken, so many end in disappointment, bitterness, and anger. We always think there is a better person or a better promise of relationship out there. Why can we not finally find that promised land?

The beginning of wisdom occurs the day we recognize the obvious—that the only person present in every scene of our still-unfolding psychodramas is ourselves. However convenient it might be to blame others for whatever has not turned out so well, we still have to grudgingly accept some measure of accountability for what transpires in our relationships. To alter Satan's lament, "Which way I flee is me." We must look to our own strategies for handling overwhelmment and abandonment if we are to understand our difficulties with other people. The first "readings" of the world, the relationships to which we were exposed, often provide the frame, the paradigm for subsequent relationships. Accordingly, they keep showing up, imposing themselves, even when we think we have outgrown them.

We have all seen couples who play out an old approach/avoidance dialectic. One experienced early relationships as invasive and thus learned coping measures of distancing and layered protection. The

> The beginning of wisdom occurs the day we recognize the obvious—that the only person present in every scene of our still-unfolding psychodramas is ourselves.

other suffered insufficient reassurance and warmth and now is forever hungry for affection and security. We can see why they might quickly become irritated with each other, perhaps even retaliatory in their intimacy. But could it be acknowledged that some part of them sought out precisely this kind of person through whom to reenact that troubled history? Why would we do that to ourselves? Why succumb to what Sigmund Freud called "the repetition compulsion"? The answer somehow has to be that we enact over and over what we know, how our relational dynamics were programmed, and we unwittingly seek even the painful repetition as something known, something familiar, something quite like "home."

STRATEGIES IN RESPONSE TO OVERWHELMMENT

In the book *Hauntings*, I employed the metaphor of living fractious adulthoods in houses haunted by fractious spirits. The earliest "stories" we phenomenologically evolve out of primary experience prove compelling, redundant, reductive, repetitive, and powerful in our lives. Thus, the messages of early relationships often show up in subsequent relationships, even those decades later. This helps explain why those who grew up under conditions and in relationships that repeatedly invaded their fragile childhood boundaries—that is, under overwhelming conditions—will develop patterns of avoidance of intimacy, compliance with the "expectant" other, or power stratagems, hoping at last to bring the environment under control.

Avoidance

Given that the core message of any incursion upon our person is that the other is powerful and we are not, we learn to avoid confrontations or engagements that put our insecure selves at risk. Among the generic paths of avoidance are many strategies: suppression, simple avoidance of anything threatening, postponement, numbing, blaming others, projections onto others, repression, and dissociation.[4] Each of these reflexive responses is a defense, the consequences of which pile up.

Compliance

Given that the social contract and the complexity of social interactions require cooperation and even sacrifice of egotistical desires, patterns of relative compliance are what make a society function. However, there are invisible zones wherein compliance rises strictly out of fear. The most common form of such compliance is the widely shared reflex called "codependence." This mechanism often passes for amiability or is praised and reinforced as "niceness." But a reflexive, unconscious choice, one succumbing to an archaic anxiety, is not nice; it isn't even a choice. In codependency, the power projected onto the other trumps our capacity for independent choice. In time, the cost of such accommodation leads to a loss of integrity, as well as to depression or anger at the loss of one's freedom. Remembering that one definition of *depression* is "learned helplessness" and another is "anger turned within," we see that codependent avoidance is a costly "protection" of the child we were.

Power Complexes

The problem of "power" haunts every relationship. Power itself is neutral, neither inherently good nor bad; it is the energy to address life's problems. But it can be pernicious when caught in a complex. As we all have learned, when power dominates a relationship, it drives out relatedness. When used consciously, however, power can be problem solving, cleansing, and efficacious.

If we examine our relational histories, we readily see these three patterns—avoidance, compliance, and power complexes—at work, as well as the accumulating consequences. Thus, the paradox, *what was once protective, now imprisons us*, is an old, old story. When we see reticulated avoidance, compliance, or power struggles in our relations with others, we may be certain that such strategies evolve from an archaic fear of the other. If we can muster the consciousness to recognize this, we might also see the other as simply "other" and not as an imminent threat. Most of us know this, and from time to time, many of us outgrow those early fears, along with their contrails of consequences; we show up in life as best we can. Others of us, however, remain stuck in our old stories like a fly in amber. If, from time to time, we recognize these patterns and are not caught in them all the time, we are "healthy neurotics." We are "neurotic" because we suffer a deep split within, but we are "healthy" because we know this and struggle with that split as courageously as we can. The future belongs to us, then, because different choices will lead to different outcomes. Those who cannot help but serve the powerful programming of the past are owned by their defenses and are stuck in history, captured in "personality disorders."[5] Their souls live in a world governed by the core perceptions and core coping mechanisms attached to the world of trauma that generated them. Sadly, as Immanuel Kant put it, out of the crooked timber of humanity, nothing can be made straight.

STRATEGIES IN RESPONSE TO ABANDONMENT

The companion threat to overwhelmment is, as we have seen, abandonment. Those whose primal experiences were characterized by uncertainty, demanding conditions, or abandonment have similarly responded with three different categories of defense strategy: low self-worth, narcissism, and neediness.

Low Self-Worth

Given that each of us began life "reading" our environment for messages, we usually consider that those messages are not only about the world but also about us directly. Putting it bluntly and literally, *What happens to me is about me and may even identify and define me.* Accordingly, if our early relationships were characterized by a sense of "not enough," we usually internalize this experience as a statement about our own diminished worthiness or capacities. Such wounds to self-esteem are common and subsequently show up in two seemingly contradictory ways. The most common is self-denigration—pervasive feelings of unworthiness or inadequacy that are followed by the avoidance of necessary choices and risks or even by self-sabotage. Or we may be caught in overcompensation: "Look at how wealthy I am," "Look how wonderful and accomplished my children are," or "Look at all my achievements." When we see these familiar behaviors, we may be sure that the person is actually acting out of a diminished sense of self-worth.

Neediness

Another response is that of being dominated by an incessant hunger for reassurance. This need can be hidden by making oneself indispensable to others. It may exude poison into the world via envy or jealousy. More commonly, it manifests in such a repetitive solicitation of the approval of others that it tends to drive others away, thus dialing up an understandable need to "neediness."

Narcissism

A third response is once again driven by the power complex and seeks control over others: our partner, our children, our employees. All of us have narcissistic wounds, but that does not make us narcissists. It does mean, however, that those core wounds often show up in our controlling behaviors with others, our passive-aggressive sabotages, or our thousand forms of manipulation.

All three of these forms of "haunting" by our earliest relationships show up in the governance systems of later life: self-denigration, inordinate need for reassurance, and a panoply of power stratagems. As before, most of us suffer these contradictions between the person we want to be and the person we are. That we are aware of this internal conflict and occasionally take a stand against these archaic behaviors makes us a healthy neurotic, a person who has hope of a larger future. Those who are owned by these core perceptions and adaptive strategies suffer the imprisonment of personality disorders.[6]

We all have all six of these existential adaptive patterns to the two wounds of overwhelmment and abandonment to some degree, and they autonomously exercise some measure of influence over our daily patterns of behavior. For all of us, life is forever flooding our fragile boundaries or giving us insufficient reassurance or love. All of us have had to devise "stories" to make these environmental factors make sense; we have then had to create concomitant strategies to cope with those stories. (If you cannot see all six at work in your own life, then I submit that they are nonetheless likely working their way through invisibly, unconsciously.) Certainly, one or more coping mechanisms, such as avoidance or manipulation of others, may have prevailed at one point in our maturation and then slipped back into the shadows as we moved to others, but they all remain and are reminders that what we see is a compensation for what we don't see. What we see are behavioral patterns; what we don't see are the archaic interpretations of self and world within each of us from whence they enter the world.

We can see from this second principle why behavioral, and even cognitive, psychotherapy, as useful as it may be, is often insufficient for genuine transformation of the personality. Until the deeper matrix, the reflexive protection system that lies below conscious thought, can be identified and struggled with, the patterning process retains its autonomy, rooted as it is in our core perceptions and survival mechanisms. Until we get below what we see, we cannot begin to understand where we really live. That is when the battle begins, often a battle for one's life throughout the length of one's life, but a battle worth fighting and winning. If you start to catch these behavioral patterns as they spill into the world, you can arrest them from their autonomous governance of your life.

III. All is metaphor.

If the human psyche is a self-regulating, self-directive system, it would be nice if said system would communicate with us in discursive language, typing out a text message, perhaps, or sending e-mail attachments informing us how to conduct the business of daily life. In actuality, it does do exactly that, metaphorically speaking. The psyche is always, always speaking to us through the various avenues open within our humanity, but it uses the language of nature. Jung was once asked if nature, as in our strange dreams, means to deceive. He replied that humans deceive, but nature, never. We have to learn the language of symbolic expression as our ancestors once knew and be humble in our effort to accept what nature has to reveal to us. Our distant ancestors lived in a chthonic world of strange, frightening, inexplicable, and seemingly arbitrary powers. But that world was alive to them, charged with spiritual energy and illusive meaning. We live in the same world, although we employ a different set of images to explain what we experience, and we pride ourselves on demetaphorizing the world into bland abstractions. (I often think that if the Japanese court poets of a thousand years ago had created the cyber world, we would have such places to visit as "the pond of a thousand lilies" instead of "hypertext transfer protocols" and "the hillside of blooming hydrangea" instead of "files and folders." At least we got the small but most serviceable "mouse" right.)

Life is inexplicable. Every time we discover something about it, it opens new avenues of exploration and unanswered questions. It is our nature to pursue these curiosities for, as Aristotle noted in his *Metaphysics*, all humans by nature desire to know. Yet, what is most desirous for us remains outside our concepts and methodologies, and the more sophisticated both become, the more elusive that smile of the Cheshire Cat. (Remember that both philosopher Kant and the quantum physicists inform us that we do not know the other; we know only our subjective, idiosyncratic experience of the other. Kant made metaphysics obsolete and depth psychology necessary, quite like modern physics rendered Newtonian physics limited and contextual.)

However, the human psyche has presented two tools with which to approach, if not to appropriate, to intimate, if not to explain, the mysteries that draw us to them: *metaphor* and *symbol*. The etymology of each tells us much. *Metaphor* means "to carry over" or "to carry across," and *symbol* means "to project toward" or perhaps "to project alongside of." Neither presumes to link us directly to the mysterious other, but both bring us into proximity to, into felt relationship with, that elusive other. When the poet compares the beloved to a flower, we know he has not fallen in love with a plant but is rather employing a more approachable and common experience of beauty in order to point toward the inexplicable allure of the beloved. While the plant image he employs is also inexplicable, we get what he means and participate in the game that metaphor makes possible. Were he instead to say, "She knocks my socks off," we also would understand and not think the poor soul is now in need of footwear. Metaphor and symbol work because we can, from both ends of its usage, appreciate and participate in the game. So, we need to recognize that our relationship to nature "naturing" is a similar invitation to a game that allows us to stand in relationship to that which lies beyond our powers of comprehension through conventional forms.

TRUSTING OUR INTERNAL MESSENGERS

The psyche is constantly registering its opinion on how life is going from its perspective, not necessarily from that of our ordinary ego's understanding of things. Our ego consciousness is often captivated by and responding to demands from the outer world, which are real and imperious but which oblige us to overrule and ignore the testimonies arising from within. Or, quite frequently, that same ego consciousness can be in servitude to a complex, a charged cluster of one's history. Earlier this day, I was speaking with a very gifted but driven and troubled man who has served well his parents' expectation of excelling in everything from business to sports. Life has at last brought him into an arena in which his skills are no longer germane or effective. He is having to reframe his experience and shift his priorities from serving his parents' expectations to finding what his own soul wants from him. The collision of these competing claims is never easy on a person. Outwardly, his life of accomplishments seemed to be his choice, but inwardly, it was driven by the need to please. Learning to sit and wait and ask what psyche might want instead is an entirely new and threatening assignment for him.

The psyche registers its opinion in multiple and plentiful ways. First of all, we have the immediacy of the "feeling function." Note that we do not create feelings; they rise from us as spontaneous, autonomous, qualitative, evaluative analyses as to how the psyche is registering the moment. We may deny these reports from the interior or repress them or anesthetize them or project them onto others, but we do not create them. If we can, quite simply, respect this autonomously reactive system, we might have large clues toward change of course. In other words, if the world or my complexes are pushing me to some sort of agenda and I serve it to the best of my ability and am rewarded with the loss of positive feeling toward that set of goals, then I have an engraved invitation to a summit conference with myself.

Similarly, the energy systems available to the psyche help us survive, but more than that, they offer qualitative information, if we pay attention. Life often demands our expenditure of energy in service to survival and adaptation. Fortunately, we can and do mobilize that energy, which is why we are still here, above ground. However, when that energy is invested in environmental demands or imperious complexes contrary to the soul's intent, we find our energy waning. We find it harder and harder to call up the effort. Enervation, boredom, depression, and ultimately exhaustion and burnout are stations along this dismal subterranean tunnel.

As we have seen, our psyche revolts and escalates into psychopathology —that is, the formation of arrow-pointing symptoms. While our culture wishes to palliate and resolve the symptoms as soon as possible, the invitation is rather to ask, *Why have they come? What is their critique? What do they want from us?* With a depression (and we all have pockets of depression while still being functional), we have to ask where the psyche would rather invest the energy from the places where the sybaritic executives in the top floor of the ego high-rise are investing it. If someone said to you to liquidate your savings and invest them in that great new company Enron or in covered wagons that are surely going to stage a revival, you would think them daft. But we often invest our precious capital, our soul's energy, in dead places every day and wonder why we do not feel that sense of satisfaction that ought to be there.

When we are doing what is right for us, something inside us supports and carries us through even the most grueling, difficult times of our life. We all have had that experience of getting through a difficult place and being rewarded by the sense of rightness, the sense of purpose, the experience of meaning that rose from that place.

All of these modalities—feeling, energy systems, moments of meaning in the midst of great struggle and pain—are examples of how we need to learn to read the "metaphoric" nature of nature coursing through us.

THE LANGUAGE OF DREAMS

In addition to these venues of communication, we must remember the critical role of dreams. Nature does not waste energy. Sleep researchers have indicated that we average six dreams per night in a normal sleep cycle. While many dismiss these nocturnal visitations as the runoff of daily events or the working through of the plethora of stimuli we experience, a humble attendance upon dreams will begin to reveal that they have a purposive nature, sometimes a compensatory nature, and sometimes a directive, developmental nature. When we are able to sit with a dream and allow its images to work upon us, we usually find it begins to percolate through the sedimental layers and take on a resonance. Paying attention to the thread of themes, assimilating the power of a particular image, listening to the resonant recognition that comes to ego consciousness—all bring us into a different relationship with our own deeper reality. We begin then to tumble to the radical prospect that there is something within each of us, some locus of observation and perspective, that is directing the production of these dreams and seeking our humbled dialogue with them. What this can mean is that our locus of authority and our obligation to report to it can slowly shift from the demanding world outside to a respectful conversation with the reality of the inner world.

Over the past few decades, I have seen thousands of dreams, and I continue to marvel at their wisdom. Hour after hour, we wrestle with these spectral presences, these opaque visitors that we all encounter. I observe that over time, tending to our dreams generates a shift from reporting only to the demanding outer world and the default allegiance to the totalitarian complexes fate gave us toward a growing sense of wonder at this mysterious, symbolic source within each of us.

Let me just cite a few examples. Recently, a woman in her fifties who had suffered serious outer losses in her life felt immobilized and stuck. In her first session, she said that she dreamt she was in her parents' home where some sinister presence had sucked some "male energy" (her phrase) down the toilet, but that energy was still alive and pulsing beneath the floorboards of the house. Such a dream is both a diagnostic picture and a prescription. First, it portrayed her loss of initiative and direction as a result of traumatic loss; second, it told her that the energy was not dead but still present. The task for both of us, then, was to attend to the process of going "down there" to recover that positive animus energy, to use Jung's term, and begin to address the summons to rebuild her life. The soul has enormous regenerative energy. While some issues within our history might never fully heal, some other energy grows around those places and enlarges us even as the trauma would define and diminish us.

One of the most memorable dreams from a client appeared very early in my practice; it was reported by a sixty-six-year-old woman who had recently been widowed. While she resisted the idea of dreams and dreaming, she nonetheless brought in a dream that had offended her. Briefly, she had grown up in another culture, a patriarchal culture in which Father's word and Father's authority were unchallenged. She knew her father loved her and meant well by her, so she voluntarily submitted her critical life choices to his thumbs-up or thumbs-down. This authority extended to his approval or disapproval of any young man who came courting her. Only when her father was dying did she transfer that authority to her new husband. While her husband was also a benign and well-intended presence, she did not begin to deal with the buried issue of personal authority until she was widowed. At first, our therapy dealt with her grief, which was real and pervasive. But when she brought the dream, I knew our work had shifted from supportive psychotherapy to analysis—namely, the engagement with the deeper currents that were seeking her development and healing, even in the context of bereavement.

In her dream, she and her late husband were on some sort of pilgrimage together. While passing through a lovely garden and crossing a bridge, she realized she had forgotten her purse. Her husband moved on ahead of her, but she had to fetch the missing object. And what do we find in a purse? One's identity, one's keys, one's resources, one's personal items—in short, a cornucopia of personal worth, facility, and identity, not to mention a basket of metaphors. Unbeknownst to the dreamer, the dream was telling her what she did not know until that point in her seventh decade—that her personal authority had always been subsumed unto the authority of others.

The dream continued with her retracing her steps. When she reached that bridge, or "transition" phase, she was joined by a man her age whom she did not know but felt was familiar somehow. Uncharacteristically, she told the stranger her life history as they crossed the bridge, concluding with her confession that her husband had recently died, and she felt so alone. He replied that he knew this and, shockingly, said that her suffering had been good for him. In both the dream and in reporting it to me, the therapist, she was offended by the impudence and insensitivity of this "stranger." But I knew it was the beginning of her encounter with that missing "male" presence that had been sucked under the housing of her life but was still there waiting to be discovered.

Once we could move beyond the literalization of the dream image of the offensive visitor to its symbolic function, she began to realize how that outer trauma of loss had also made possible the discovery of the inner energy that she had until then vested in the two paternal figures in her life. From that trauma and the recovery effort, I am pleased to say that her last years were full of new life, travel, and personal development that would never have happened otherwise. Her previous life had been productive and, by all conventional standards, a life of achievement in the professional arena, but it was also not wholly hers. It was a life lived in servitude to the well-meaning instructions that came from others. Only when that external presence was lost could she begin to discover a relationship to an inner authority that had been there all along. The capacity of the psyche to heal itself, to express both the problem and the agenda for growth in symbolic forms, has been and remains a miraculous engagement to me. We do not invent or create these things; they are working within us to serve and support the work of nature.

We see by these examples how the psyche always speaks to us. It speaks through the venues of body, of mind, of dreams, of intuitions, and it speaks symbolically. If we knew, as Jung once argued, that there is a two-million-year-old person inside of each of us—a presence bearing the wisdom of nature, the directives of the soul—would it not behoove us to pay attention to that personage, indeed, to cultivate a relationship to it? Would it not make sense to pull out of the cacophonous din going on outside us at all times and

> The psyche always speaks to us. It speaks through the venues of body, of mind, of dreams, of intuitions, and it speaks symbolically.

the tumult transpiring within to get in touch with that presence? But we are all, as Jung pointed out when he was still an undergraduate at the University of Basel, so terrified of encountering the still, quiet, but knowing voice of the soul within. It is so much easier to perpetuate the paradigm of childhood: tiny, dependent, and expecting the large "other" to make sense of it all for us.

This flight from personal authority is the legacy of being so utterly alone and dependent, and it completely ignores the possibility that nature, or divinity, instills in us the requisite tools for surviving and for making our way. The other animal species arrive "knowing" what they need to know. We do, too, but we are socialized and separated from that primal "knowing." Until we have exhausted our efforts to find that authority "out there," we are unlikely to risk hearing what has been a quiet thunder within us from the first hours of our unsteady passage on this earth.

Even as an undergraduate, Jung had a remarkable awareness of this presence within him, even as he decried the noise of the world around him. (What would he have made of our 24/7 wired culture of immersion in external stimuli?) As he put it,

Every moment of our lives is trying to tell us something, but we do not care to listen to this spirit voice. When we are alone and still, we are afraid that something will be whispered in our ears, and so we hate the stillness and anesthetize ourselves through sociability.[7]

What, we now must enquire, might be whispered in our ears that is so troubling? What might be asked of us? Isn't it easier to remain small, dependent, and forever searching for the "other" who will spare us that risk? Easier, perhaps, but as we shall see, not satisfactory.

To us as creatures of habit and reinforced patterns of defense, change is both risky and essential in getting our lives back again. What is metaphoric here is how we carry over the defense of one time to another, as well as how we prejudice and limit our field of choice in doing so. We think we are responding to the immediacy of this present hour when we are actually enacting an old story, an old version of reality, and transferring it to this later hour. And thus, in time, we convince ourselves that this is who we are and what the world is, rather than how our story keeps repeating the same old, same old. We can, however, awaken to these outdated metaphors through the metaphoric language available to us in dreams, through the symbolic messages from our own minds and bodies, and through literature.

5

Antigone, Hamlet, and Prufrock: Case Studies in the Search for Personal Resilience

As we have learned, we always resist our life circumstances in due proportion to the anxiety that ambiguity, change, and uncertainty generate in us. Overcoming such resistance is a psychological task, as well as a spiritual task, because it involves not only crises of anxiety arousal but also crises of values. So, let us look at some of these psychological issues in specific "case reports" taken from the field of literature rather than from the annals of psychiatry. In three literary prototypes, brought to us by Sophocles, Shakespeare, and T. S. Eliot, we see people not unlike ourselves caught in in-between moments in their lives, seeking a point of reference for guidance, and finding (or failing to find) the resilience to carry them through. All of us live in multiple in-betweens in our lives and our yearnings. The ancients knew this well, as do the giants of Western literature. So let us remember our comrades Antigone, Hamlet, and Prufrock and apply the substantial gifts of depth psychology to the archetypal journey we share with them.

Antigone, as we shall see, lives between her obligations of citizenship and her respect for the gods, between her desire to fit in, to be acceptable and secure, and her love for her broken brother. Hamlet lives in the terrible gap between what he wishes to do, what he needs to do, and his capacity to do the necessary. J. Alfred Prufrock lives in the gap between self-images—that to which he aspires and that which he in fact lives; in the abyss between desire and the courage to act on that desire. Sounds familiar, doesn't it? Don't we all suffer those same needs, those same desires? Yet, we live in the quotidian, the adaptive, the avoidant, and we suffer the Hell of neither here nor there, the purgatory of lost souls.

In 1930, T. S. Eliot, a self-proclaimed Christian poet and critic, praised one of the most countercultural of nineteenth-century figures, Charles Baudelaire. Eliot noted that Baudelaire, the author of *The Flowers of Evil (Les Fleurs du Mal)* and other confrontational texts, was not one of the trimmers of Dante's Hell, one of the half-committed; on the contrary, he was spiritually strong enough to merit Hell rather than live in the twilight zone of non-being. Baudelaire's spirituality was honestly earned, not the received authority of others. As Eliot concluded,

> So far as we are human, what we do must be either evil or good; so far as we do evil or good, we are human; and it is better, in a paradoxical way, to do evil than to do nothing: at least, we exist. It is true to say that the glory of man is his capacity for salvation; it is also true to say that his glory is his capacity for damnation.[1]

But most of us, most of the time, live in the netherworld, the world of the in-betweens.

When we examine the psychology of these in-between spaces, these liminal zones, we see that we have already left the past, or it has left us, and the future is not yet apparent or realizable. Many times, for example, the decisions to end a job or a marriage have been made in the unconscious long before, are abetted by a progressive withdrawal of energy, and then appear as semiconscious behaviors, finally percolating upward into consciousness. And while we could be grateful for that clarification of our situation, we often are frightened, even paralyzed, to be on such uncertain ground. Our uncertainty, our grasping of the old known and secure, even when limiting or abusive, often keeps us stuck for a while, as we saw in chapter 4. Even when the decision has been made in the deepest realms of our soul, the executive function of the ego is often intimidated, and we collude with our stuckness. As miserable as we may feel in the hole we have dug for ourselves, we choose to stay there for a very long time. At first, our plight arises out of our unconsciousness, and then out of our flight from knowing what we already know, and then from our failure of nerve to move into the unknown future. To reach the future, which is just as real as our past, we have to consent, or be driven, to be out of contact with the old for a very long time. No ocean is ever crossed without that willingness to risk, to leave behind the known shoreline long before the new land is found. As Jung expressed succinctly, "If you want to cure a neurosis, you have to risk something."[2]

ANTIGONE'S DILEMMA: THE IN-BETWEEN OF CHOICE AND CONSEQUENCE

From time to time in each of our lives, we face truculent choices, the consequences dire no matter what we choose. How may we discern what choices are right for us, and how may we face their consequences? Sophocles' 2,500-year-old drama brings us back to the conundrum of choice and consequence each of us faces in our quite different journeys.

There are two different lenses through which to view *Antigone*. The first is informed by what one might call the "tragic vision of life," as embodied in the classical imagination of ancient Greece. The second is the ever-contemporary "dilemma of choice," which embodies the conflict between "received" versus "personal" authority.

For the ancients, the "tragic vision" was a sophisticated understanding of the perils and promises of the human condition, a psychology before psychology as we know it existed, seeking to address this question: "How is it that I set off in that direction for my life, with these intentions, and wind up in this quite different place, with these quite troubling consequences?" Their answer to this question remains germane to our lives and to public events unfolding in today's news reports.

First, the tragic vision identifies a *force field of influence* blowing through all of us, directing, defining, limiting—a set of "givens" over which we have no control. Among these determinative forces are the psychodynamics of our families of origin, our received genetics, and the social, political, cultural context into which we are born—all of which have the power to define us, limit us, and direct us. Their word for that directive force was *Moira*—Fate! Similarly, there is a force field blowing through us that seeks its expression *through* us, seeking to become and using our puny lives as its vehicle. Their word for this developmental drive within each of us was *Proeirosmos*—Destiny!

And last, they observed the role that *we* play in this convergence of energies and identified three dimensions that speak to *our* accountability for how our lives turn out. The first dimension is something inherent to each of us—what the ancients called *character*, a predisposition to certain choices, recurrent proclivities, and particular consequences. Second, given that we all intuit our tiny, vulnerable state in a vast and overwhelming universe, we often overcompensate, arrogate to ourselves powers we do not in fact have. Thus, we think we are in charge, that we know enough to make proper choices, that we can foresee consequences and pretty much manage our lives. This presumption, this arrogance, they called *Hubris*; in psychology, we call it *inflation*. In truth, we *never* wholly know enough to know enough, and we are always caught up in a web of consequences deriving from our choices, however well intended they once were. Third, they recognized that we all make choices from a flawed perspective, from the distorting lenses ground for us by culture, family of origin, and the vagaries of our personal biographies. As Kant observed, if we wear blue spectacles, we shall see a blue terrain with only blue choices. This refracting vision, this biasing of our choices, they called the *Hamartia*, sometimes translated as "the tragic flaw," or as I would put it "the distorting lens." So, we never see through the dark glass clearly; instead, we are prone to choose only what our refractive lenses permit us to see.

How natural it is, then, that we find ourselves in a world of consequences rising from the choices we have made, little knowing the complexity of forces operating on our consciousness at the time and unable to foresee how it all will play out. As our ancestors perceived, we all live "tragic lives," not because our lives are dark and full of doom, but because we are obliged to choose in a contingent world in which our powers of discernment and freedom of choice are far more constrained that we ever imagined. Enmeshed as he or she may be in this web of consequences, the tragic figure is humbled through suffering, comes to consciousness, and is brought back to right relationship with the gods. So humbled, he or she is in a better position at the end, more nearly in right relationship to the gods and their mysterious will than in the beginning of their unconscious arrogance and imagined sovereignty.

Most of us know the general outlines of the story of Oedipus, a guy who found a girl just like the girl who married dear old Dad. Sophocles presented this story of the House of Thebes in three plays, *Oedipus*, *Seven Against Thebes*, and *Antigone*. After the dethronement and apotheosis of Oedipus, a civil war rends the body politic and casts brother against brother in bloody contention. His sons, Eteocles and Polynices, die in the fraternal war. The ruling monarch, Creon, declares that the former will be buried with honors and the latter degraded as a traitorous rebel and left to rot unburied and desecrated. The surviving sisters of the warring brothers, Antigone and Ismene, are torn by their divided loyalties. Antigone defies the dictate of Creon. She buries her brother Polynices out of respect for him and for the rites due the gods. Ismene is equally loyal to the memory of her dead brother, but she is much more compliant, much more intimidated, much more afraid of crossing Creon's declaration. As she says,

> I needs must do, but yield obedience
> To them that walk in power . . .
> I was born too feeble to contend
> Against the state.[3]

And Antigone is not naive about what her choice portends:

> I shall meet with nothing
> More grievous . . . than death, with honor.

When we have to pay with our lives for our values, can we be so certain that we will hold to them as Antigone did? What would we choose? And why?

Each of these figures gets locked into a rigid position, as we all do when we are triggered by a *complex*—that is, by some cluster of our own energized history. From the insights of depth psychology, we have learned that we seldom are truly choosing consciously; instead, we are often under the influence of historic forces that we have internalized or are responding to environmental pressures we little suspect have such influence over us. (We have known since the 1980s from brain studies that we typically make choices unconsciously, reflexively, even *before* the ego world becomes aware of the necessity of choice.)

This dilemma of choice is our second consideration. What dictates our choices? Most of the time, we respond to life's demands in routinized, conditioned ways. We find patterns piling up, seldom remembering that each is the product of a set of specific choices made by us—the only person present in that long-running drama we call our lives. Our patterns of avoidance, our ready compliance, our power drives—all come from our complexes, whether operating consciously or unconsciously within us.

Moreover, whenever we have to make difficult choices, we unwittingly stumble over the hidden problem of "authority." By what authority do we make our choices? Someone else's model or our free choice? Which part of us made that choice—the truly conscious part (assuming we are ever *wholly* conscious) or one of those clusters of energy that are so familiar yet so autonomous in our histories?

When it comes to how we behave externally, most of us most of the time obey the clues, admonitions, instructions, and threats that we received from our family of origins, or we follow the educational or religious directives and generally serve the social contract into which we are born—*even* if they violate the intent and integrity of our own souls. As Jung put it, all neuroses are experienced as "conflicts of duty" or conflicting authorities colliding within us. Think of Socrates. When he was unfairly, but legally, condemned to die by the state, he submitted to the state as he believed a loyal citizen should, and he willingly drank the hemlock.

Antigone arrives at one of these terrible junctures in her life and is forced to make a life-altering, life-threatening choice. When she is caught between her loyalty to the city-state, to the cultural norm, to the received authority and her own inner authority, she suffers.

Similarly, when her civic duty and religious fealty collide, she is the unwitting victim at the intersection of those values.

Antigone is obligated by her civic duty to obey Creon and deny her brother's rebellious body the dignity of a burial. She argues that in addition to fraternal loyalty, she has a still higher obligation to obey the expectations of respectful burial as demanded by the gods. Yet, what a slippery slope that is! Every psychotic who commits an act of violence, every fanatic who in an unreasoning way imposes upon others, or any one of us in the grip of a powerful complex that brings harm to ourselves or others is an example of the undifferentiated, easy impulse of the hour, buttressed by a rationalization to make it justified. Only when a person suffers through these dilemmas, only when he or she holds out until the legitimate claims of both sides of an issue have been affirmed, only when he or she is willing to suffer the consequences—as Martin Luther King Jr. did in the Birmingham jail and Dietrich Bonhoeffer did in a Nazi concentration camp—can one lay claim to "right" judgment in the face of these tormenting opposites.

As Jung said, holding the tension of opposites until "the third" appears is the only way to work our way through to the choice that is right for us. The "third" is what that choice means for the psycho-spiritual *development* of the choosing individual, especially when called before large opposites in their life. And always, the willingness to accept the consequences of one's choice is the hallmark of a mature decision.

So, while we count Antigone as a hero of conscience, where does that leave Creon? Antigone is the *heroic* figure, and Creon the *tragic* figure. He is not a bad person. He is charged with captaining the ship of state and serving as its custodian. In defending the integrity of the state, he proclaims,

> She [the state] is our ark of safety . . .
> Such are the laws by which I mean to further
> This city's welfare.

But when his law and order authority are challenged by Antigone's act, he is enraged and driven to order her execution in the full flush of his complex. His rigidity, his capacity for arrogant presumption, and his absolutism result in ruin for his lineage. He intimidates dissenters and needs to see his own will reflected back to him. One can even imagine him proclaiming himself the most popular person in Thebes, with the largest public support, and the largest crowd ever at his inauguration. Still, in the end of the drama, only he is changed through the humbling that brings insight. Antigone remains resolute, while Creon gains insight through what Aeschylus called "the awful grace of God."

Quite telling is the witness of the character Tiresias, allegedly a blind, hermaphroditic, transgender seer who always speaks the truth but who, like Cassandra of other Greek legend, is seldom believed. In *Oedipus Rex*, Tiresias says, "it is never reason not to listen to reason." But when do any of us listen to reason when we are in a complex, in a mood state, when we are caught up in the fever of the moment? When Tiresias tacitly supports Antigone's position, saying that it is the will of the gods that the dead be buried with respect, Creon accuses him of "fake news," of corruption, and rejects the seer's sobering advice. This is Creon's tragic error, an error that rejects what Kierkegaard called "the teleological suspension of the ethical," which honors a commitment to the transcendent rather than to the merely civic. Similarly, when offered counter advice from his own son, Haemon, Creon erupts out of willful pride at this affront to his absolute sovereignty. Tiresias is sent away, his counsel of prudence unwelcome. Speaking of Creon's rage, the prophet says,

> Let him vent his spleen on younger men,
> And learn to keep a tongue more gentle, and
> a brain more sober, than he carries now.

Sometimes, it seems, neither wise counselors nor family members nor reassigned generals can keep mad kings from self-destruction. Creon's manic defense of his position costs him his son; his wife, Eurydice; and the good will of his people. In winning the game of thrones, he loses all that matters. As the Chorus reflects, his destruction is

> unwrought by the hand of others,
> But fore-caused by his own self-will.

Driven by impulse or complex, Creon sets in motion the tumbling chess pieces that bring all to ruin. His tragic flaw is not his insistence on the primacy of civil law but in his hubristic assertion of his power. Remember the Greek maxim, "Nothing to excess." Creon's intemperance, his rage, his unquestioning conviction of his own righteousness—this is his flaw. He arrogates to himself a righteous position as defender of civic order and produces further civil division and polarization. Inevitably, the gods drive large chariots through these gaps in our psychic armor. All things, the gods' will, come back into balance in the end. Wherever there is excess, the deep leveling forces of *nemesis* (consequences), *sophrosyne* (temperance, prudence), and the many other powers in the nature of the universe exert their compensatory will and bring us, like vain Icarus in his arrogant flight, back to earth. Or, as Jung put it in terms that chill me always, "What is denied inwardly will come to us in the outer world, and we call it *fate*."

The intent of the tragic vision was not to crush humans but rather, through the testing conflicts of opposites, through the redemptive forge of suffering, to bring them to wisdom. On the night of Dr. King's assassination, Robert F. Kennedy paraphrased a quote from the conclusion to Aeschylus's *Agamemnon* in a speech to a crowd in Indianapolis:

> And . . . in our sleep, pain which cannot forget,
> falls drop by drop upon the heart, until in our own despair,
> against our will, comes wisdom through the awful grace of God.

Thus, a potentate in his palace, a tyrant in his tower, is nothing compared to the higher state of the humbled who, at last, has come to right relationship to the gods. The greatest of sins is *hubris*, narcissistic inflation, the sundry seductions of power or privilege to think we are more than we are. In the end, all of nature, all the gods, all of our psychic processes reveal a leveling power. Where castles stood, ruins survive; where arrogance reigned, humility prevails. As the Chorus in *Agamemnon* concludes, the gods in the end bring

> Great blows on great speeches
> And deal with a Boaster . . .
> teaching us [all], wisdom at last.

Antigone, imprisoned in a cave, takes her life. However, she sticks to her values not out of arrogance but out of submission to the will of the gods. Creon perishes in the judgment of his contemporaries for choosing his own egoic will over the wisdom of humility, and he brings down his empire, the state, his family, and his power in that leveling that in the end comes to us all. So, in this theater we call *history*, in this unfolding plot we call our *lives*, populated within, as we all are, by our own contentious characters, let us learn what the gods have been trying to tell us for such a long, long time. Their reminders of our limits reach across the millennia to each of us and call us to a new mindfulness of what is not conscious but is playing its willful way through us all still.

HAMLET: FIGHT, FLIGHT, OR FREEZE

What can be said about *Hamlet* that has not already been said many times? What can I add to what is now a classic and perhaps even a cliché? Did you ever see the cartoon in which two elderly theatergoers walk out of their first production of *Hamlet* and one says to the other, "That Shakespeare was so intelligent." And the partner replies, "But he's overrated—all he did was fill his play with famous quotes!"

But *what* has made *Hamlet* a classic—that is, a work that continues to speak through disparate and desperate times and through the undulating tides of popular taste? *Why* does it continue to touch us? Let us remember that despite the depth and range of Shakespeare's vision, his plays had to be commercial successes, as that is how he made a living.

Hamlet endures in our imagination because his "stuckness" is so familiar. He is caught between "complexes," each laying claim to his choice, and each producing consequences when not chosen. Hamlet's complex problem, and often ours as well, is that he "knows" what is right for him, what he has been called to do, but for reasons he knows not, he does not so act. Recall St. Paul's *Letter to the Romans*, in which he says, "Though I know the good, I do not do the good."

Why, we ask? Paul, not knowing much about the unconscious, attributes this contretemps to *akrasia*, a Greek word meaning "a dilatory or insufficient will." Today, we know there are splinter agencies, half-formed personages, haunting our psychic interiors and exercising a will of their own, a will independent of the knowledge or control of an ego consciousness so easily usurped. Hamlet's problem is so common because we share with the melancholy Dane a fractured psyche swarming with shadowy personages that have not been introduced to each other yet, and if they were ever introduced, they would not get along with each other very well.

I think it is fair to say that *Hamlet* is the first truly modern text, and Hamlet the first truly modern person. Despite the passage of four centuries, Hamlet is so familiar to us because he knows, really knows, that *he is his own worst problem*. (As do we.) He knows he is stuck with himself. (As do we.) No amount of blaming others, no whining, no petitioning the gods will spare him from himself. While Shakespeare called the play a tragedy, it seems that it may more accurately be considered a work of irony. In tragedy and comedy, redemption occurs, whether through the insight that suffering brings or the release that laughter brings. In both tragedy and comedy, the cosmic order is restored. In the ironic sensibility, there is recognition and insight but without redemption, without restoration, without growth. In *Hamlet*, each character sees, understands, and is face to face with his or her own limiting contradictions, and yet they are each unable to convert that suffering into action, into change, into transformation. They remain stuck, as so often we remain stuck, so often deepening the hole in which we find ourselves.

As we saw earlier, psychoanalysis works with people trying to get unstuck by surfacing the internal "psycho-logic" by which they are stuck. So too, we must also remain stuck unless and until we find the secret logic of our stuckness and face the anxiety that getting unstuck will bring to us when the resistance is overcome. At least we have a shot at moving from psychic paralysis to action. Learning from our brother Hamlet is one way to reflect more deeply on our common dilemma.

Let us look more carefully at Hamlet's context. The Danish kingdom has been rocked; the king, murdered; and the queen, remarried to the dead king's brother. While one may praise the speed of reassurance of a firm hand on the helm and the continuity of government, such a tumultuous event will be more than disconcerting to Hamlet, a college student summoned home from his frat house in Wittenberg, Germany, a city that Shakespeare's audience knows full well has also been shaken by the challenges to the accepted order by a young monk named Martin Luther. In addition to sophomoric angst and hormonal turbulence, young Hamlet is dismayed. Not only is he orphaned by his father's death, but his mother has quickly transferred her allegiance to what he considers "incestuous sheets." He dallies with the thought of ending his turmoil out of loss, guilt, and shame, were there not Divine prohibition against suicide.

Other disturbances are afoot. For one, the guards have witnessed a ghostly presence on the ramparts of the castle, an itinerant spectral presence whose agitation is evident. Hamlet joins the guards at the castle walls, where the ghost of his father appears and reveals that, in fact, he was murdered, poison poured into his ear, and that his wife has married the murderer. (This may prove even more disconcerting to a student than having Dad's check bounce on registration day.) Shaken as he is, Hamlet knows the ghost and his testimony are authentic. It is up to Hamlet to avenge his father's murder and his mother's betrayal. All of Denmark would support and approve such righteous revenge, and yet for him, understandably, the whole earth has shifted. Nothing he knew or took for granted is the same or stable. He says, as we might,

> The time is out of joint—O cursed spite,
> That ever *I* was born to set it right![4]

All a college student wants is easy classes, a date for Saturday night, and fiscal backup from home. But this? This? Who would want to deal with this in-between state of things?

Resolute as he is, Hamlet understandably is aswarm with conflicting emotions, wishing personal escape from the conflict even more than he wishes justice. In his most famous musing, we hear echoes of the sort of misgivings, rationalizations, evasions, and resignations that we all know so well in our own lives.

To be, or not to be, that is the question:

*That is, do we enter the terrible tumult of this world, or do
we find a way to evade its painful demands on us?*

Whether 'tis nobler in the mind to suffer

The slings and arrows of outrageous fortune,

*That is, to roll over, go with the flow, and
slip slide away into another day.*

Or to take arms against a sea of troubles,

And by opposing, end them. To die, to sleep—

No more, and by a sleep to say we end

The heart-ache and the thousand natural shocks

That flesh is heir to; 'tis a consummation

Devoutly to be wish'd.

*That is, to slip back into the sleep of childhood, to get stoned, to
feel no pain. But, what if we are not left alone even then?*

To die, to sleep—

To sleep, perchance to dream—ay, there's the rub,

For in that sleep of death what dreams may come,

When we have shuffled off this mortal coil,

Must give us pause. . . .

*Ah, the dream of modern America: all is well, all is well, did we
not have bad dreams. If only we could escape to fantasy land,
embrace a blissful afterlife, make America great again, but . . . .*

But that the dread of something after death,

The undiscover'd country, from whose bourn

No traveller returns, puzzles the will,

And makes us rather bear those ills we have

Than fly to others that we know not of?

The Devil you know is better than the Devil you don't know.

Thus conscience does make cowards of us all,

And thus the native hue of resolution

Is sicklied o'er with the pale cast of thought, . . .

And lose the name of action. (emphasis added)

From four centuries ago, this is a perfect description of a complex—a part of ourselves dissociated from the ego, operating autonomously, that has the power to shut us down. All of us have some primal fear, some archaic terror, some forgotten but still-carried memory of the powerful, traumatic Other that shuts us down, stops us dead in our tracks, generates the archaic "fight or flight" patterns that we lament but that never leave us. "The pale cast of thought" is Shakespeare's way of describing the ethereal yet palpable presence of an energy that removes our executive agency; freezes us in the same old, same old; and leaves us stranded on the desolate beaches of familiar stasis.

Many, if not most, young people flounder in the uneasy state of late adolescence/early adulthood, when the brain is still knitting its hemispheres together and the ego is awash in hormonal baths and impulse-driven behaviors. Parents know not what to do, often thinking that their addled youth are mad, insufficiently grateful for their privileges, and a general pain in the ass. If any one of us can look back upon those turbulent years without regret, embarrassment, or chagrin, then he or she had an exceptionally bland history or was perhaps stoned that whole time and just does not remember. It's a wonder that any of us get this far in life; most of us arrive here by dumb luck or the grace of the inscrutable gods.

There is no single Hamlet, no definitive reading of him. Each age has seen him anew as a protean Rorschach, perhaps projecting their own needs, their shadow, and their blind spots upon him. Naturally, I will not avoid this trap myself and will offer a view that I have already introduced. If I am influenced by my day job as an analyst, so be it. I see the Hamlet in each of us. Who among us has not, from time to time or even every day, fallen into a complex of some kind wherein we serve the script, the directions, the outcomes of our personal and cultural history? Who among us has not dallied, compromised, postponed, rationalized, blamed another, or distracted ourselves from the bloody business at hand? Who among us has not recognized that what is most wrong in our lives rises from us? Who

Who among us has not turned away from what we knew in the depths of our soul we were summoned to do?

among us is armored through life's daily collisions with unwavering self-esteem, ready talents to take it on, and the resolve to push through what life throws in our face? Who among us has not known resistance, inner division, swirling and contradictory motives and agendas? Who among us has not turned away from what we knew in the depths of our soul we were summoned to do?

That Hamlet does all those things so familiar to us, that he knows he is accountable for how it turns out, and that he is a prisoner less of outer circumstances, though they may be many and powerful, than of himself, his own personality—all of this makes him our contemporary. If Hamlet screws up his life, so do we. If he gets up off the floor and tries to take it all on again, so do we. It is not much of a stretch to say, then, that Hamlet is our brother.

Hamlet's plight is much like ours. We never fully have the real story, never achieve crystal clarity about what is going on, but we are still called to act as if we know and understand. And if we mess it up, then we are part of the same human club. All Hamlet asks of us is that we remember him. So, let us then hold him in our hearts, hear his story, and be recalled to our own unfinished business at the same time.

PRUFROCK: A SONG NEVER HEARD ALOUD, A MAN FOREVER BETWEEN

> Do I dare
> Disturb the universe?
> In a minute there is time
> For decisions and revisions which a minute will reverse.[5]

The Love Song of J. Alfred Prufrock was written between 1909 and 1911 and published in 1915 by T. S. Eliot. Only 500 copies were printed, and it took seven years to sell out the first edition. Today, it is considered one of the most important poems of the twentieth century—a poem of original style and a great psychological portrait of a person wedged in a great in-between. The poem depicts the terrible in-between of desire and inhibition, riven by the knowledge that might liberate but only lacerates, by the song that is to be heard in the world but never will. If this is a love song, it is a song of love's defeat, regret, stasis, and enmeshment in a netherworld. Prufrock is just trying to get through, just like us, or just like parts of us; he is adrift in a world larger, more powerful than he can ever be. He constantly compares himself to others, having learned, as every child does, how dependent he is on the approval of others. He doesn't like himself very much, as most of us don't. He knows too much, but none of that knowledge will liberate him.

The poem begins with an epigraph from Dante's *Inferno*, the speech of a character who speaks freely to the visitor from the upper realm whom he believes is also in Hell with him and thus cannot spread the story of his shame in the upper realms. It is a confessional spoken sotto voce to the reader, a person whom he presumes is also in the self-constructed Hell of eternal consequences.

Prufrock's name alone reveals his ambivalence. *J. Alfred* is a bold declaration, and also pretentious, perhaps inflated. His surname implies something effeminate and constrained: *prude* and *frock*. Throughout the poem, images of in-betweenness emerge: an "etherized" walk through twilight fog to a tea party; the recurrent emergence of a critical "question" that is never asked; the gap between his constant comparisons of himself to heroic figures (Michelangelo, John the Baptist, Lazarus, Hamlet); the desire to talk with a woman and the fear that she will reject him as insignificant, even laughable. In every venue of his life, Prufrock finds himself caught in the gap between desire and aspiration and limitation, fear, and shame.

He wishes to step into life, and yet, he repeatedly finds time, not as the arena for being but for "a hundred indecisions, / And for a hundred visions and revisions." Compared to his heroic aspiration, he concludes, "I have measured out my life with coffee spoons." He suspects life is too much for him and concludes that a vegetal, unconscious life would be better than this life of self-flagellation.

> I should have been a pair of ragged claws
> Scuttling across the floors of silent seas.

So emptied is his sense of self that he imagines that even Death will consider him a poor harvest.

> I have seen the eternal Footman hold my coat, and snicker,
> And in short, I was afraid.

In life's vast psychodrama, he wishes he had at least the heroic struggle of Hamlet, but the best role that he can assign himself is that of Polonius, the ridiculous old man full of clichés and pomposity.

Prufrock never breaks through, never steps into the heroism of living his own life, pursuing his desires. Instead, he feels like an insect, a drowning person, a figure of ridicule. Trapped in his skin, trapped even more in his fears, and trapped still more in his "stories" about himself, he never taps into that nature-given resilience that lies within and that can carry us through the most difficult of times.

While scholars have discerned that so much of both "Prufrock" and "The Wasteland" reflected Eliot's own psychological struggles, his descriptions are so familiar because they echo so much our own self-denigrating behaviors, our constant looking over our shoulder to see what people are thinking about us, our incessant cursing of how our dilatory will resists what we know we want to do with our lives. In an era that has dethroned the heroic vision of life and replaced even the tragic vision, we are left with an antithetical profile of the antihero: the daily struggle to make do, slipping further and further behind, blaming ourselves, blaming others, hoping others don't figure out what a wreckage we are. If Hamlet is our brother, Prufrock is us—or at least a good part of us.

The archetypal dilemmas of Antigone and Hamlet call forth the tragic vision of life. Please remember that life is not "tragic" because we die; we die because we are natural creatures. The tragic vision is a perception of our timeless struggle with the gods, our endless endeavor to wrest meaning from this short visitation on a perilous planet. The tragic figure is not guilty for this aspiration; as we saw before, the tragic figure is guilty of only one thing: hubris, presumption, inflation. As rich, sophisticated, and generative as our thinking may be, in the end, wisdom is found in our alignment with nature, not in our "defeating" nature. Thus, the tragic hero or heroine is richer in the end, though in "defeat," because he or she has come back to right relationship to the gods. The oldest of sins is presumption: Adam and Eve, Prometheus,

Oedipus, and so on. As Aeschylus wrote millennia ago, the gods have ordained that it is through suffering that we come to wisdom, the wisdom of realignment with the will of the gods. Whenever we cavil at this notion, we begin the step into that ego inflation that leads to ultimate undoing. In the tragic vision, wisdom is found in humility, not in inflation or arrogance.

> As rich, sophisticated, and generative as our thinking may be, in the end, wisdom is found in our alignment with nature, not in our "defeating" nature.

REVISIONING THE GODS OF OUR OWN PSYCHODRAMA

In the tragic vision, the gods are remembered, respected, and allowed their godly ways, ways often inexplicable to the limited minds of humans. Among Jung's many comments on this matter, perhaps his famous and peculiar definition of *God* illustrates his profound respect for mystery. Shortly before he died, he was asked by a reporter for the U.S. magazine *Good Housekeeping* what he meant by *God*. He replied, "To this day God is the name by which I designate all things which cross my willful path violently and recklessly, all things which upset my subjective views, plans and intentions and change the course of my life for better or worse."[6] One will not find a definition like that in any organized religion, nor in the conception of most folks; however, it is both challenging and humbling at the same time. It reserves for the gods their sometimes terrifying autonomy, the inexplicable mystery they embody as they move through the world and the human soul, and it summons us to remember our due proportion and to remain humble.

The tragic experience is active suffering, active wrestling with the Angel of Darkness as Jacob did. The opposite form of suffering is pathetic, arising from *pathos*—"suffering," but passively. Prufrock knows enough about active suffering: he sees it in the work of Michelangelo, Hamlet, and others. He, however, whines. He curses his fate and thus sabotages destiny, that which might have been possible for him to embody in this world. Tragic suffering has depth and dignity and is a spiritual virtue; passive suffering is, well, pathetic.

Much of our lives is spent in the in-betweenness that irony describes so well. We know but do not do; we understand but do not change; we kvetch but do not become. Why? Fear, as Prufrock suggests? Yes, much of the time. Lack of imaginative possibility? Yes, all of our complexes and psychic drivers are limited in their purview, which is why, again, we must take seriously the correctives of dreams and psychopathology.

In viewing these portraits in pathology, the range of choices, the permutations, dilemmas, wiles, confessions, failures and triumphs, self-deceptions, and occasional moments of enlarged consciousness in literary characters, we add to the range of *our* understandings, *our* modes of expression, and *our* possible freedoms.

If we recognize ourselves in the dilemma of Antigone and know the paralysis of fear, we are still summoned to be persons of value. If we remember Antigone only, and sometimes with sentimentality, because she won her way through to the clarity of truth and stood before the gods in humble respect for the truth, we must also remember how easily Creon fell into the old and tawdry power complex, the final refuge of the weak. If we see in Hamlet's resistance to doing what life asks of him a familiarity with our own slip-sliding away, our own endless shabby supply of excuses, we also learn that *in the end, only action will redeem*, not stasis or in-betweenness. If we recognize in the tergiversations of Prufrock our own prolongations of risk and commitment, at least we know that Hell can be here and not in some dismal otherness. And if we don't like living in Hell, perhaps we can muddle our way toward risks that lead to a different world, rather than spend an eternity in suspension.

Each of these literary portraits are "case histories," and we are further chapters, or perhaps footnotes, to each of them. What our story will finally be and how our soul's unfolding turns out still depend on us to show up and risk stepping into what our journey asks of us.

6

What Is Healing?

What is healing, and what can we do to further its work in us? If it is on each of us to further our own healing and that of the world, what is the scaffolding of nature's restorative process, and what is the intent and movement of the soul's work? What role do we have to play in all this? How can consciousness and learning assist or impede this process?

My last book, *Living an Examined Life: Wisdom for the Second Half of the Journey*, laid out twenty-one tasks, the addressing of which will lead to a richer, more satisfying life. It was, and remains, my contention that those tasks, assignments, summonses are at work within us, whether we know it or not. Our consciousness can aid them, just as our flight from thoughtfulness around these matters can undermine them.

Among those twenty-one tasks were these critical assignments for healing:

- *Recovering personal authority.* We all have personal authority at the beginning; it is called *instinct*. Our bodies know what is right for it, our souls know as well, but our adaptations so often split us off from the primal knowing and lead us to distorting life strategies. Any choice that arises out of deferred personal authority will likely prove wrong for us in time.

- *Assembling a mature spirituality.* Our spirituality is as mature as our character is mature. What role does fear management play in the deformation of our spiritual life? Does our spirituality preserve the mystery of the

Mystery, or is it a subtle attempt to create images and practices that ratify our complexes and keep them reassured? Does our spirituality make us uncomfortable enough to require that we grow up and grow onward, or does it perpetuate the sleep of childhood?

- *Choosing meaning over happiness.* "Happiness" as a state of being is wholly contextual, unique to each person, transient. We can no more achieve a permanent happiness than we can predict the weather months from now, because happiness is not a place, not an abiding attitude or state of being.

These are but three of the tasks identified from a long list of accountabilities. Such accountability means that we assume partnership in our mental, physical, and psychological well-being. A sense of the rightness of our life doesn't just happen to us; we are partners in the ongoing conversation that calls us to show up and be responsible. Just as groups are no more evolved than the level of consciousness of the least of them, so our well-being is no more evolved than wherever our neglect of ourselves is keeping the whole from moving onward.

One of the things I observe in the contemporary world is an increasing awareness that something is not right. We have, generally, the living conditions for which our ancestors longed, and yet as a culture, we are swimming in malaise. More and more folks are tumbling to the notion that *they* are going to have to decide what their life serves—how they can gain a sense of purpose, find emotional satisfaction from their labors, and value something more than power, wealth, and security. More and more people believe that they have to be as fearless in their choice of a life that makes sense to them, rather than fit in, please others, or serve cultural expectations. Recently, I was talking with a former student who left his very high-paying job in a financial corporation in order to retrain as a social worker. He said I told him at the time of that decision that he would pay a price either way, but the price of regret would be far higher than the price of tuition. He is now in the work of sitting hour by hour with people in distress, and he would not trade it for the world. He took that risk, leaped into his own abyss, and found that something within rose to support him, carried him through, and rewarded him in a new way.

For any of us to find that purpose, to be served by the resilient powers of nature, we have to heal. We were close to the source as children, but then, day after day, those necessary adaptations began the long exile from our psychological homes. Healing will involve returning to ourselves, the selves equipped from the beginning by Divinity or nature, replete with resilience, desire, and nature's resources of strength and endurance. After all, nature wishes us to survive, and more than survive—it wishes us to serve Being by becoming that which is wishing expression through us.

As I reflect on the healing process, I think of the following seven general principles. Some are obvious; others, less so. They are as follows.

1. We are equipped by nature to survive, live our journey, and become.

Admittedly, this particular animal, the human, is the most complex and needs the longest length of protection before it is able to manage on its own. Some animals arrive and minutes later are fending for themselves. We all forget, however, that nature brings us here with the requisite resources to survive. As Rilke put it to a nervous young poet's querulousness, we are set down in life in the element to which we most correspond ourselves. Yet, as we all know, nature is not enough to get us through all the obstacles. We also need the blessings of fate to support us sufficiently until we can manage for ourselves, drawing increasingly upon the resilience that nature provides us.

2. Because of our powerlessness, we must adapt, and so we create "stories" to help us understand.

Among our management systems is our imagination. Life itself is a big blooming profusion of stimuli so immense that we can never understand or absorb it all. This particular animal responds to the inherent traumata of life via the imagination. We are meaning-seeking, meaning-creating animals. Thus, we attempt to make sense of our experience, to understand the world in order to better survive in it. In doing so, we imagine fractal "stories" seeking to answer the questions of survival. "Who are you?" "What is that?" "Is it safe or hostile?" "How can I live in the face of that?" Our "stories" arise from trying to make sense of our life, to make it predictable, perhaps more manageable. And, of course, the stories are the product of the limits of our imaginal capacity as children—constrictions of time, place, cultural lens, and other delimiting factors. The "wrong" stories can turn us against ourselves. In time, we can outgrow many of these stories as we accumulate other experiences with a different slant, but the earliest stories persist and thread their way through our entire lives.

3. We become servants of and prisoners to our "stories."

Given that our stories are efforts to interpret the world and make it more knowable and more manageable, we come to depend on them to carry us through ever-new situations. The good news rising from our stories is that often our "interpretive fiction" allows us to build on our knowledge, bind our days together, and have a reasonably coherent personality. The bad news is that those same stories also impose the paradigm, the limited and limiting lens of the former onto the immediacy of the new. Thus, we create patterns, whether intended or not, and we become prisoners of what we depend upon. Even when we find our choices and their subsequent patterns problematic, even destructive to us and others, we perpetuate them because they are familiar, perhaps because at that hour they are the only way we can see the world. This leads to the "repetition compulsion," which over a lifetime dots our histories with stuck places, blockages, and replicative reenactments.

It is, as I pointed out before, so hard for any of us to realize that we are not what happened to us. What happened to us was an external manifestation by fate, but our story about that is uniquely ours. So, if the child interprets the neglect as a statement about his or her worth, rather than see that the deficiency was really that of others, then we can

It is so hard to realize that we are not what happened to us.

expect either a lifetime of self-sabotage, unworthiness, and lack of permission, or a grandiose overcompensation—both driven by a faulty narrative around what a fated encounter ostensibly meant. It was never about us, but it is our story, so we remain influenced, if not governed, by it.

Much of our lives are governed by what logicians call "the fallacy of overgeneralization." What appeared to be true then is imposed over and over on other situations, creating a provisional verification of the original interpretive fiction. While we sometimes outgrow these stories, most of them—those involving phenomenological encounters between self and other and the traffic in between—persist in our lives. We can see why, then, psychotherapy in later life involves working backward from the texture of our histories to identify the operative narratives, lifting them out and into consciousness, and challenging them with a larger frame of reference and enhanced resources than the child ever possessed. Indeed, reflection, therapy, and insight allow us the critique of our stories; they begin to separate us from our history and restore a connection to the internal sources of guidance.

4. Without the gift of psychopathology, we would never be stunned into an awareness of the need for reconsideration, and thereby perhaps transform to a larger "story."

The tenor of modern life is deeply vested in the idea of management and control. Our vast armamentarium of tools, from computers to modern medicine to ever-expanding technologies, feed the fantasy of increasing control over our lives, even as other aspects of our lives slip more and more out of our control. We must always remember that the human ego consciousness, which arrogates to itself vast presumptive powers, is rather a fragile wafer floating on a tenebrous sea. I have recently heard the following ego rationalizations: "I know what I think." "I have no shadow." "I am quite conscious." And as a humorous sweatshirt I saw said, "I know I am right. Don't you think I would know if I weren't?" All of these assertions beg the question, "What do I not know that is in fact running my life?"

Fortunately, we are reminded again that we are "gifted" by psychopathology. What a strange statement that is, in the context of contemporary Western culture. How is psychopathology a gift? When we remember that the literal meaning of psychopathology is "the expression of the suffering of the soul," we then begin to get a clue as to how this "gift" functions in our lives.

I have already described how our "stories" help us adapt, adjust, cope with the magnitude of life's incursive demands on us. This species survived when parallel branches perished in the evolutionary smithy precisely because of its adaptability to ever-changing circumstances. Consider that if we were only creatures of adaption, without autonomous souls, then we would simply be creatures of habituation and channeled energies and values. If, for example, we were instructed, as in fact we all are, on how to live our lives and in service to certain values and we had no soul, then the fulfillment of those instructions would be all that life would ask of us. But we possess an autonomous region of the psyche that apparently has its own agenda and expresses its displeasure when our adherence to our external assignment contradicts its intent. We can, and needs must, occasionally mobilize our energies in service to survival, regardless of the calling of the soul; over time, however, adherence to a set of aberrant assignments leads to escalating commentary from within. The more my ego focus insists on a certain behavior or commitment under the domination of an external claim or possession by a complex, the faster my energy is depleted, the more the body aches, and the less and less meaningful it all seems.

Psychopathology is a gift, then, because it gets our attention. It tells us that the soul is not pleased with where our energies are going. It seeks corrections of course from the executive-branch decisions, and the more we resist, the sharper the messages grow. The weight of our societal obligations is huge, and the power of our earliest stories of adaptation and conflict management is extraordinary. Hence, the power of the psyche's expressions of dismay must grow apace. For us to simply medicate them away or rationalize them is to push the summons to alternative choices into a deeper hiding place.

5. Psychopathology calls us to accountability to something larger than "palliative" care.

In speaking recently with a man whose entire life has been governed by the demands of a very narcissistic parent, he complained of his anger leaking out inappropriately in situation after situation. This leakage derives from the vast cellar of anger he carries at having been enslaved to the power techniques of that parent. It is easy enough to say move away, act differently, and he has. But we also have to recognize how that early story of powerlessness before the demanding giant told him he was doomed to fruitless suffering. I reminded him that two functional definitions of *depression* are "anger turned inward" and "learned helplessness." As a child, he got the indelible message that the giant Other was impermeable, devouring, and relentless. So, he learned helplessness, and he turned his legitimate anger back upon himself, the only one he had permission to assail. Predictably, a history of depression and self-medication emerged as a by-product, sequels to a once-accurate story but a story long outgrown.

The central theme that threads through the second half of our lives is accountability for whatever the first half produced. (I use the term "half" of life in its psychological, not chronological, sense. The second half can begin as one faces aging and mortality or the death of a loved one or a thousand other moments when we step back and begin the radical reassessment of our lives.) The first half of our lives is pretty much a large but necessary mistake as we enter the world thinking we know who we are, what we want, and what is important to devote ourselves to. Some of those choices are quite appropriate and bring enduring meaning to us, such as caring for our children; other choices are driven by our response to external pressures or our "stories." And thus, we bumble into and through life, but somewhere along the way, the psyche keeps knocking on the floorboard of our flimsily constructed psychic dwellings and gets our attention. Then, hopefully, we have acquired enough ego strength to bear looking at the topography of our lives, and for sure, we will have accumulated much to observe by then.

As obvious as this encounter with ourselves seems, not everyone shows up for the appointment. Kierkegaard told of a man who was astonished to find his name in the obituary column of the morning newspaper, suggesting that he did not know he had died because he did not know that he had lived, either. So much of our life is on automatic pilot that we all risk waiting until the end to try to figure out what this life has really been about. On that note, I have noticed with my clients seventy and older the many, many dreams that survey their histories. In some cases, one might conclude that those distant events still contain residual energy, perhaps unfinished business; but I also think that the psyche is deliberately parading our life before us in order to get us to better see what the drivers have been, the operant stories, the remaining tasks of assimilation, self-forgiveness, and continuing vigilance. It might behoove us to awaken while we are still here, still writing our story on those remaining blank pages. Failure to do so consigns the sovereignty of our lives to our demanding histories. What profound sorrow must arise from this failure to be the bearer of being that seeks expression through us. What life asks of us, how we are to carry it forward, how we are to serve it—all this is left empty and discarded. As Rilke counseled the young poet, everything is gestation and then bringing forth. And what if we do not bring forth what wishes to be born from us? As the gnostic *Gospel of Thomas* observes, if we bring forth what is within us, what we bring forth will serve us, and if we do not bring forth what is within us, what we do not bring forth will destroy us. Those are pretty harsh statements, but they are millennia old and from someone before us who reached this same conclusion of accountability.

6. Our central tasks are recovery of permission, personal authority, and personal aspiration.

The emergence of depth psychology comes as a response to the summons to personal accountability. This book is in service to the same summons. As defined more particularly in *Living an Examined Life*, central to the recovery of one's more authentic conduct of one's life is the recovery of permission, the recovery of personal authority, and the recovery of personal aspiration. Each depends on the others for strength.

One of the by-products of the immense discrepancy between us as nascent beings and that of parents, powers, and myriad principalities is that we overlearn our essential powerlessness. We realize that our well-being depends in large measure both on the generosity of those entrusted to our caretaking and on our capacity to meet the conditions our fate brings to us. History is full of worthy souls who were crushed by the weight of slavery, abuse, racism, sexism, and other forms of denial of their soul's right to expression. We may only grieve their suffering and unlived possibilities, but we may be resolved to live whatever remains to us to the fullest.

To grasp those possibilities for fuller life expression, we need first to wrestle with this deeply implanted, archaic hold that the old power discrepancy between the outer world and the inner word, to both of which we are obliged to report, still has on us. This shift of our center of gravity begins by asking less what happened to me than another question: *What wants to enter the world through me?* That we might be the bearers of new life into this world is the only antidote to the old world and its "stories."

Assuming that we can ask that question and consider its implications, then we ascertain that we can no longer afford to live tentatively, *as if* this were our life. We can no longer ask permission to believe what we believe, desire what we desire. We have to seize permission. It is not given to us. It is an act born of insight, occasionally courage, sometimes desperation. Permission to accept our destiny is now a greater summons than the gravitas that fate weighs upon us.

Second, we have to sort through the immense internal traffic we all experience in the information-jammed, invasive world in which we live. Which threads of narrative come from our old stories? (And to address that question, we have to know something about the presence of those invisible agents in our daily life, presences making decisions for us, frequently eating our lunch for us.) Further, we need to identify and begin a dialogue with those intimations that also come to us from the soul. We have many of them but have lost track of them in the thicket of choices daily life demands; we are often intimidated by the third step—finding the courage to live them in the world, with all the consequences that may bring us. Those moments of decision and commitment are both terrifying and exhilarating.

Third, we have to recover the dreams and imaginings we left behind, long ago and far away. Because of changes in the body, and because of time's closed doors, we can't recover all of them, but many, in some form or another, are within reach still. If only we had permission! At this point in life's journey, surely we can ask ourselves, *What am I waiting for? Do I think my parents are going to show up on my doorstep and punish me? Do I think the loss of approval from others will forever sabotage me? Do I think it will still be too much for me to take on?* What fears? What old narratives? What? Is it not time to set them aside before they write the final chapters as they have written the previous ones?

Recovering our interests and aspirations, valuing them, is surely the best hope we have for recovering that sense of wonder, curiosity, joy, and fulfillment we occasionally grasped as children. Our nature is there to serve and support us in those hours of decisive commitment to grow, to change. What are we waiting for—Elvis to show up and say, "Yes, you can have your life now"? Reportedly, he left the building some time ago.

7. The project of growing up is to keep working to heal the splits within until we serve what is wishing to enter the world through us in the first place.

It is not the role of the ego to choose those aspirations. They are chosen for us by our natures or by the divinities, whichever story makes more sense to you. It falls to the ego to decide what to do about these callings. The splits we carry are debilitating, painful, regressive, and they have the power to immobilize us or direct us to all sorts of palliative efforts. Yet, something within us always knows what is right for us, and its insistence on expression is what keeps us awake at night, nudges from within amid our busiest hours, or causes us to envy others for what we see in their life that we have not brought into our own. If we are truly living our life to the best we can, risking the things that matter most to us, the lives of others will never be a distraction or source of envy. Neither will we be preoccupied by self-doubt. We will be too busy taking care of our business to be distracted by such deflections.

Healing is the act of nature. But we can assist that process by respecting what wishes expression through us, even if the world around us does not. Do not think, as we often did as children, that if we are outvoted by that noisy world, then we are wrong. We are simply outvoted. Throughout the world, crazed and crazy people clamor for our attention, for our votes, for our spiritual allegiance. If we are ever going to be true to our own voice, it has to be now, while there is still time.

If we are ever going to be true to our own voice, it has to be now, while there is still time.

If *healing* is an act of supportive nature, *vocation* is a summons of the soul. What larger picture, what unrealized possibilities are destroyed when we do not embody that which wishes expression through us?

The work of healing begins by attending to the soul's desire for expression.

As a Near Eastern sage once wrote, it is as if we were sent to this land with a royal assignment, and if we have only dithered about and forgotten our task, then we have violated our reason for being here. Each of us must remember that we were sent with the gift of our personhood, and if we fail to embody that in the world, we have failed our mission.

Whatever the impediments life brings—social, physical, mental, spiritual—the soul is forever seeking to work its way through all barriers, not unlike that blade of grass that emerges from the concrete imposed upon it. The work of healing begins by attending to the soul's desire for expression. Recall that the word *psychotherapy* means "to listen to or to attend the soul." Thus, the work we do to attend the soul's intent is called "healing."

This summons for accountability for our own healing has long been recognized. One especially plangent voice expressing such desire for healing comes again from the nineteenth century: Matthew Arnold in his poem so aptly titled, "The Buried Life."

> But often, in the world's most crowded streets,
> But often, in the din of strife,
> There rises an unspeakable desire
> After the knowledge of our buried life;
> A thirst to spend our fire and restless force
> In tracking out our true, original course;

A longing to inquire
Into the mystery of this heart which beats
So wild, so deep in us—to know
Whence our lives come and where they go.[1]

The buried life *is* buried but still alive. It remains to us to risk pulling it up into realms of consciousness and lived experience. We did not have much say over how and why we got so separated from ourselves, but we certainly do have some say about how we bring ourselves back together again.

7

The Maiden with No Hands:
A Psycho-Mythic Interlude on Gender

In the United Kingdom and the United States, we read what are called "fairy tales," although no fairies inhabit their realms. In Germany, they are called *die Märchen*, which simply means "the Tales." They are the carriers of folk wisdom, and for such reason, they must, in some way, satisfy over the generations because they speak to or replicate the organizing structures of our brain. Such stories appeal, despite their local apparel, to the trans-local, psychic substrata that organize and drive us all.

To see another example of a person like Antigone, someone caught between values systems, between loyalties to something large and compelling, we turn to the tale "The Maiden with No Hands." While the tale speaks of timeless issues, the version I draw upon was gathered and edited by the Brothers Grimm in 1810 precisely because this vast oral tradition that provided psychological continuity and folk wisdom—sometimes also called "tales of the spinning wheel"—was eroding as Western culture moved to cities, to machines, and, most of all, away from the oral tradition to the era of packaged information.

THE WOUNDING OF WOMEN

The tale begins with a miller who is sitting in his front yard, impoverished and depressed. Since we don't think about what millers do—namely, grind grain to produce flour and bread—this profession is alien to us. Our ancestors thought of a miller as a "trickster," a guy looking to cut corners, make a buck; tricking, as he did, the nearby stream and waterwheel to do his work for him. Then the Devil appears. It has been asserted that the Devil works his way so well because he knows how to say exactly what we wish to hear. He tells the miller, "I will make you rich if you simply promise me what is in your backyard." When one con man meets another, he assumes he can con the con man, and so the miller readily agrees, knowing that there is only an apple tree in his backyard, an object of little value, little loss. But he is unaware that his daughter sits under that same apple tree, and thus, his daughter has been bartered for material gain. The miller and his wife, poor in more ways than one, are suddenly flooded with material wealth.

When the Devil comes to lay claim to his purchase, she declines to go with the Devil but yet submits to her father's deal, caught between loyalties like Antigone. When her inherent goodness proves sufficient to sabotage this demented bargain, the Devil insists as his penalty that her hands be cut off. She submits, and the mutilation occurs, but at least in respecting the father's bargain with evil, she is not in servitude to the Devil. In time, a well-meaning prince pities her; they fall in love, and out of sympathy, he makes her silver hands. As well intended as these appendages are, they are artificial and not really useful. When she gives birth to a lovely child, the Devil spreads the word that she has given birth to a monster and orders her to be killed. She names the child *Schmerzenreich*, which can be translated as "Full-of-Sorrows." To save herself and her child, who is her potential for future growth, she retreats into the forest for seven years. Her plentiful tears drop daily onto the stumps of her arms, and the hands slowly grow back.

When we consider this wounding and healing, we observe that the healing does not come from the helpful prince, nor from an external male or patriarchal agency. Only time, suffering the wound, and the regenerative tears derived from the original fluid in which we floated and from which all life comes offer the healing agent. Her healing comes from her true mother, not the wife of the miller, who is pleased with their newfound wealth, but the Great Mother, the archetype of nature that is forever seeking to heal itself. When the prince comes upon her in the forest after that exile of seven years, they fall in love again and marry. This kind of sacred marriage is often called the *Hieros Gamos*, or "holy marriage," the uniting of opposites in one's psyche.

While the wounding of the maiden, and other women, is grievous indeed, sometimes a part of life can be lost to us but its meaning still found and transformed. Often, in the place of wounding, our greatest insights, our developed talents, our compensatory energies emerge out of psyche's resources.

This story has often been seen, and quite appropriately, as a parable of patriarchal wounding that severs women from their natural roots. Just ask most women in executive positions what happened to them, psychologically, in getting that title on the door and then ask them what they now find missing in their lives, what aches career success has brought their souls. This patriarchal wounding can be perpetuated even when women are in those high offices because this dynamic is not exclusive to gender as much as it is to the distorted equation between the values of power and relatedness. Jung pointed out that wherever power prevails, love is driven out. Systems that feed on competition, zero-sum outcomes, and dominance over cooperation and mutuality are servants to power over relatedness. Women who find themselves in such systems suffer all sorts of symbolic—which is to say, psychological—mutilation.

One such former client was a highly successful corporate executive who was grossly overweight, chronically pill-popping, and subject to dreary, persistent moods. Her very drive took her away from her greatest gift, which was her inherent compassion and ability to see what others needed and to help them find that.

We are currently witnessing the rise of compensatory energies to the one-sidedness of history. Jung's simplest definition of *neurosis* is the "one-sidedness of the personality." What has been more one-sided than the domination of the patriarchal world, with its power complexes, its hierarchies, its destructive competitiveness, its oppression of women, for sure, and of men as well? As we witness the progressive dismantling of this teetering one-sidedness, the task will be to integrate the so-called feminine values with the so-called masculine values. I call them "so-called" because each gender carries the opposite within. So, if I am to access my "feminine" aspects, they are but part of my masculine totality, even as a woman can, and must, lay claim to her "masculine" values. What has so labeled them and split them is also the source of this problem. None of us was born with this split in our personhood. But to replace the patriarchy with a matriarchy will only be neurotic in another direction. Valuing the "feminine" and the "masculine" equally is the only path toward greater wholeness and fuller humanity. It is clear that the healing of the maiden so grievously wounded by the greedy patriarch is underway, but her many tears already shed are not yet enough. Much work in the liberation of humanity remains, and action will be required in addition to tears. That action begins with each of us as an individual as we withdraw judgments of each other and seek the integration of these disparate gifts within ourselves better than we have before.

THE WOUNDING OF MEN

Interestingly, we can take this same tale and look at it as a parable for men's wounding as well. While the ego tends to interpret dreams from the standpoint of day-logic—namely, that things are what they appear to be—what happens when we look at the various characters as dramatizations of intrapsychic values, differentiated energies within a single person?

Ask most men what success is, and they really won't know, though they spend their lives seeking it. Let us look at the miller as the typical, lazy, opportunistic ego that would like to find an easy road to riches. Again, the Devil embodies our shadow, what we want to possess without having to pay for it. So, what gets mutilated is the inner feminine, what Jung called the "anima" in men. The anima embodies his relationship to his instincts, his feeling life, and his spiritual values—all of which he finds he cannot afford to embrace lest he prove vulnerable and lacking in competitiveness. As a result, most men live horribly isolated emotional lives, feeling shamed and unworthy and always one down from somebody else. They know, or believe, that their worth as human beings depends on their productivity, their meeting of quotas—making money, scoring points, serving abstract expectations.

Women have little idea how much shame, doubt, and self-loathing men carry within them. Even other men do not know this about each other. Thus, the isolation and self-destruction deepen. And how can a man ever have a good relationship with the opposite sex, or with his brothers, if he has such a troubled relationship to himself?

Sooner or later, most of these men at midlife or later find themselves in a dark wood, captured by a dark mood, and clueless as to how to recover. Again, the only path of healing is found "in there," in that threatening place where no outer solutions can help. Others can't fix them, so they have to learn to grieve their own estrangement and begin, like a child, to value their feeling life, instinctual life, and spiritual life again before they can recover any sense of genuine agency and personhood. Many an unwept tear lies in the souls of men. Until that healing elixir can flow, the mutilation will never heal.

THE WAR WITHIN: ANIMUS AND ANIMA

Jung's term for the inner "masculine" of the woman is the "animus"—her sense of personal empowerment, legitimacy in a world of gender constrictions, permission, sense of capacity, and willingness to risk her full expression of herself in the world as it lies before her. The "negative animus" is that voice so many women know that whispers, "Who do you think you are?" "You can't do that!" "What makes you think that is for you?" The negative animus has the power to shut her best self down, and it usually does. Similarly, the "negative anima" of the man floods him with undifferentiated anger and debilitating depression, which he treats with self-medication, redoubled efforts in the outer world, or frenzied efforts to connect with the "feminine" outside himself; he often winds up feeling more alone, more shamed, more hopeless.

Sadly, to flourish in any system is to risk disconnecting from that magnanimity of which the soul is capable.

> Whatever we deny within ourselves will come to us sooner or later and demand payment. Then, we are forced to repair within and seek healing from our own nature.

Jung, again, pointed out that people will do virtually anything—anything!—to avoid facing themselves and avoid facing the largeness of life that the soul demands.

When, however, the fury and frenzy of ego strategies grow exhausted, the psyche reasserts itself. As Jung noted, whatever we deny within ourselves will come to us sooner or later and demand payment. Then, we are forced to repair within, as the handless maiden did, and seek healing from our own nature and its restorative capacity. Given that so much psychotherapy today often supports and reinforces the ego's demands or seeks our better adaptation to the mutilating world around us, we can see why it is so ineffective. What we will not do voluntarily either will make us servants of the Devil's agents who are found all around us or will someday drag us to our appointments with the unlived life. The *Hieros Gamos*, or sacred wedding, at the end of the tale of the handless maiden is the integration of opposites; as such, it represents a portrait of healing and of potential wholeness. That's when we get ourselves back again.

8

Navigating Changing Times

Nobody can counsel and help you, nobody. . . .
Delve into yourself for a deep answer.

RAINER MARIA RILKE

We make choices every day. From whence come these choices? We wish—we believe, even—that they are the best product of our rational, conscious selves, but how did we get so far off course? Why do we not feel the rightness of our lives? But the real question is, from where in the unconscious, or from where in our history, do those choices come? Is their effect merely the adaptive protection we once needed, or do they truly serve the enlargement of our journey? We can hardly be making wise choices if we are driven by various elements—discordant parties and contending agents—in the unconscious. To recognize that one does not really know what tributaries flow into our choice making is the beginning of wisdom and the summons to greater self-scrutiny—possibly, even to therapy.

Surely, Rilke is wrong in the citation above, we protest. Do we not expect counselors of whatever stripe to help us? Are they not paid to do so? Have they not learned what we need to learn in their schooling and professional experience? Do not some of them possess special information, tools, magic to help the rest of us out of the doldrums? To get our juices flowing again? As far as that goes, who knows, really, what is the right course for anyone?

These questions naturally raise the issue of "authority." By what "authority" do we believe what we believe, value what we value, and choose what we choose? As mentioned earlier, most cultures consigned the authority to the gods and to those who interpreted the will of those gods. Intermediaries, from shamans to village elders and from soothsayers to well-coifed televangelists, assure us that they have a pipeline to the transcendent powers and have been deputized to share that information with the rest of us, as long as we pay the requisite compensation, of course.[1] What has happened over the millennia, and with increasing rapidity over the past decades, is the erosion of that received, institutional authority. Swamped in scandals, sordid money deals, and, even worse, growing indifference, these institutions have lost their sovereignty and unquestioned authority. Recently, a police officer, raiding the confidential files of a cardinal in Houston, was asked if it was problematic to challenge ecclesiastic authorities; he replied that they were treating the situation "in the same way we'd treat . . . a criminal enterprise."[2]

But the big puzzle remains: why do we distrust ourselves so much that we have to turn to other authorities? Certainly, it is true that our instinctual guidance knows what is right for us, but in childhood, we learn how dependent we are on others for our safety, nurturance, and well-being. That message, overlearned, gets transferred to situation after situation in our lives, and we find ourselves always looking to the world "out there" for clues as to what is acceptable, what not, and what permission we have to be who we are. We know a child soon learns to "read" a tilted eyebrow, a raised tone of voice, what is spoken and not spoken; all children grow hypervigilant. While this tool of hypervigilance helps us perceive and adapt to our environment, with our eye focused only on "the outer," it also separates us more and more from ourselves.

More than half the work of depth psychology is recovering an elemental trust in our deepest sources of knowing.

More than half the work of depth psychology is recovering an elemental trust in our deepest sources of knowing. While the cacophony of voices, both outer and inner, is louder and louder and incessantly present, so too is the voice of the soul, buried as it may be amid the tangled communication cables that cross our senses the same way buried cables cross the depths of the oceans. Sorting through them is a lifetime's work, and it never ends.

To this day, it is puzzling to me why so many other psychological schools of thought and practice do not work on this issue of authority more often. For example, very, very few will ever bother to ask you if you dream, nor do they receive your reported dreams with respect and attentiveness, nor do they remind you that the dream is a visitant from your depths and not simply another, lesser "ego" dealing with frustrations and fears left over from daily life. If we had dreams alone, what our ancestors often thought were messages from God or sources of revelation, we should all be astonished by the simple fact that there is something in us that "knows" and may in fact know us better than we know ourselves.

When I was in training in Zurich, I had to make some very important life decisions. What I wished was occasionally clear to me, but the path before me, not to mention the risk of hurting others with my choices, was daunting. After a typically dreary, rainy, overcast winter, I emerged from therapy just as the sun was peeking through the clouds, and I could guess that spring was, in fact, going to come again and that I was right to move forward. Even more important, I had just processed one more dream with my analyst, a dream that carried that same, insistent message. Moreover, ever cautious against presumption or being directive, my analyst leaned back and said to me, "I now believe that this is the best course for you. And you should not feel guilt because there is a law higher than the demands on the ego." While I only sporadically followed his helpful recommendation, I did feel the proverbial feather tilting the whole scales of the cosmos.

SACRIFICING SELF-IMAGE FOR SELF

In 1949, analyst Erich Neumann published his book *Depth Psychology and a New Ethic*. In this book, Neumann asserted that what we now know about the deep Self, the world of psychospiritual reality that lies beneath the ego constructs, requires us to weigh the presence of the activity of that Self in all our decisions. By no means was he endorsing narcissism or self-absorption or casual disregard of legitimate social and relational claims upon us. But, he said, decisions based only on an observance of the social norms, the group ethic, have led to the violation of generations of souls. Only a painful, sustained, and thoughtful suffering of the conflict within can bring a person to respect what the Self is seeking through his or her choices.

Around this same time, I recall being transfixed by an ancient Greek sculpture of the flaying of the satyr Marsyras in the *Kunsthaus* of Zurich. As I wandered through the galleries over many visits, I always wound up standing before that time-ravaged sculpture. Marsyras had found a flute and, flushed with hubris, challenged the god Apollo to a contest. (Let it be said that the gods may not win every contest, but that is probably the way to bet.) Naturally, or perhaps supernaturally, Apollo won the contest. To punish his hubris, Marsyras was tied to a tree and flayed alive. That was the statue whose numinosity kept calling me. I realized in time that that outer image was resonating with an inner image. Marsyras was my ego consciousness, my professed understanding of myself that was undergoing crucifixion.

In his challenging nineteenth-century book *Fear and Trembling*—a title inspired by St. Paul's comment that we are to work out our salvation in fear and trembling, or humbly and not through inflation—Kierkegaard reached a conclusion analogous to that of Neumann a full century later. While the language Kierkegaard uses is theological, its implications are profoundly psychological, revealing again the wisdom of the scriptures when we understand them in forms psychologically accessible to our sensibilities.

Taking as his parabolic frame what he called "the scandal of Abraham and Isaac," Kierkegaard proposed to interpret what such a paradox might mean to moderns. Putting it bluntly and literally, if you saw your neighbor with a knife at the throat of his child, you would call the police or intervene directly, and rightly so. But how is it that Abraham is a patriarch of the faith in reward for such a heinous act? Kierkegaard identifies three layers of social, ethical, and psychological dilemma and decision making. The first level at which most of humanity operates is what he called "the aesthetic," by which he means the narcissistic, eudaemonistic behaviors we see every day—the choices made from selfish interests, choices made from pleasure-seeking, pain-avoiding agendas. Through maturation, the self-absorbed may mature and evolve into the second level, "the ethical," whereby he or she recognizes the legitimate claims of the social contract, the accountabilities we have to each other.

But lastly, he noted, we may also be summoned to "the teleological suspension of the ethical." As we saw with *Antigone*, this is a transcendence of the merely ethical on behalf of a still higher calling—Divinity or one's own soul. Kierkegaard concludes that the meaning of this otherwise barbarous parable is that Abraham is called to determine what his highest value was. To consider that, he also was called to consider sacrificing what was most dear to him, his own child. In other words, Abraham was called to the crucifixion of his ego values. In my own life, such a crucifixion was really not about the choices before me—they were clear—but rather about the sense of self I wished to cling to about myself. Sacrificing our most precious self-image is always an invitation to a junction that none of us wishes to reach but that often comes to us in this journey. The goal of a self-satisfied image of ourselves is sacrificed to a teleological, purposeful, mission assigned by the gods or by one's own soul.

We all know what a slippery slope that constitutes for any of us. We all have witnessed, in ourselves or others, how one can justify almost anything to ratify the salient complex at any given motive and rationalize its righteousness even much later. But the key here is in the title, *Fear and Trembling*. We are asked to acknowledge how fearsome these choices are, this risk of being true to our soul, and to tremble in the face of what that acknowledgment will ask of us. Fear and trembling ask of us a genuine process of waiting rather than impulsivity, of valuing the opposites represented in our dilemmas, and then the willingness to allow what we had thought and believed pass for something else for which we hadn't bargained. Who would ever go there, to these difficult junctures, willingly? Sometimes the external world takes us to those places as it did with Bonhoeffer, who left a secure position teaching in New York City to return to his beloved Germany to stand against the Hitlerian regime and in time become its martyr. Sometimes, this juncture is approached because the Self is engineering such a meeting, where something *in us* pushes us into a place where we are obliged to move beyond the simple rights and wrongs of social life, beyond the places of comfort and predictability. Thus, Bonhoeffer's toughest ordeal was not opposing the Nazis. His values were clear. It was choosing between his sincere pacifism and his recognition that ending Hitler's tyrannical regime was the higher good, the teleological suspension of the ethical to which his life had theretofore been devoted.

In those dark hours, the luminosity of the Self is often hard to discern, but it is the only light to guide us on the path yet to be undertaken. Nietzsche once said that before the path can be followed, one must first have found the lantern. And the lantern (or Emily Dickinson's "compass"[3]) can only be found after a conscientious submission of ego sovereignty and a purgatory of fear and trembling. It is certainly understandable why the timorous ego, that wafer floating on a large, tenebrous sea, would prefer avoiding these difficult junctures or wish to rid oneself of the burden of such a summons, whether through pusillanimity, rationalization, projection onto others, or some form of somnambulant narcosis. We all have multiple evasive strategies that we have been practicing since the fretful precincts of childhood. But we do not get to choose whether life, the gods, or the Self will call us to those hours where, like Oedipus, we find ourselves in the wilderness where three roads diverge. Which to choose, and what the price?

It is in those difficult times that the larger journey is forged in the alchemical smithy of the soul, a place where the heat grows until the lesser molecules transform and the larger emerge. From time to time, the will of the Self transcends the needs of the ego-world and often requires the sacrifice of our most cherished values. One remembers the words of the carpenter of Nazareth, "Not my will but Thine." Those who have gone through that transformation have been to Hell and need not fear it anymore; they know that life will bring further tests but will not allow them to settle back into the old, familiar place. From that point onward, they live with a deeper integrity and are less and less defined by the old fears or the many hysterias found all around them. The price and the often grave consequences are compensated through a more profound experience of meaning, whether or not it is ratified by one's tribe. This is a step into our own journey that, sooner or later, we are all asked to take.

THE VITAL CLUES OF OUR NATURE

Earlier in this book, we touched on the elemental systems that nature, our nature, provides us to bring guidance in a world of bewildering choices. In sum, they include the *energy systems*, which rise to support us when we are tracking correctly for ourselves and that ebb and drain off when we are not. While we can compel those energies, and sometimes need to, we cannot sustain them over time, lest ennui, exhaustion, depression, or self-medication follow in sequence. The *feeling function* autonomously, qualitatively evaluates our experience and weighs in with its opinion. Again, we may repress, split off, or anesthetize that insurgency, but we do not create it. Thus, we can be doing all "the right things," as defined by our culture, our parents, our complexes, and the feeling function still does not sustain the investment. It doesn't "feel right," we are forced to admit. And then we have a profound divergence between ego agenda and the autonomous Self at work.

As our ancestors knew and respected, we have those internal events, those spectral presences, that occur in our lives every night: dreams. Sleep research tells us that if we live until the age of eighty, we will spend six years of that time dreaming. Surely nature does not waste energy, and this activity thus serves nature's purposes. Those of us who pay attention to dreams know that by tracking their images, themes, associations, and analogues, we often find that they are commenting on our lives. Yes, they employ mythopoetic language rather than discursive language and thought, but they are never delusive if we can step outside the narrow frame of ego understanding and open ourselves to the world of symbolic expression. Again, only symbolic expression can open us to the vast mystery in which we swim at all times.[4]

Our collective disconnect from these vital clues and our obligations to report to the demands of the culture around us separate us all from the vital sources that our ancestors and other animals knew. (As Freud put it so succinctly, "The price of civilization is neurosis.") None of our predecessors were free of fear, for life is dangerous; none were exempt from suffering and mortality. The conditions of life they had to survive were harsh and unrelenting. But few, if any, became enemies of themselves as we do; few split themselves off from their internal forms of guidance; few devoted their lives to such abstractions as economics, ideologies, and artifices, such as we all serve without counting the cost. Let this not be taken for a nostalgic desire to go back to earlier times; that is not going to happen. But it does mean we can at least begin to pay more attention to the authorities that lie within ourselves if we wish to choose more consciously. So much of modern life is in service to the loudest demand at the time, the charged complex it activates from our history, and the need to keep pace with a culture careening over the edge into a new darkness.

Perhaps most elusive of all, yet most important a source of internal guidance for each of us, is our continued monitoring of our life experience regarding its experience of meaning. We can serve the drives for power, wealth, status, relational security, oblivion of consciousness, whatever, but we cannot create meaning. Meaning is a by-product of being in right relationship to our souls at critical junctions. If what we are doing is right for us, no matter how perilous the path, we are supported from within; our suffering, our investment, our uncertainty are rewarded with purposefulness. This cannot be faked, and over time, even the most troubled of journeys seem rich with meaning.

Obviously, what is meaningful for one person will not prove so for another. While parents, well-intended institutions, and others are keen to tell us what path will prove meaningful for us, they really know neither the labyrinthine twists and turns of another's soul nor the path that wishes to unfold from within. Many times I have had to challenge the good advice of well-meaning people in telling someone what to do, simply to affirm a person's right to find that out for themselves. After the trial and error that accompanies all choices where information is partial (and this describes most important life choices), sometimes we simply have to blunder our way into our path.

In the end, the challenge to any of us regarding this internal dialogue is whether we can learn to trust, over time, what comes from within; mobilize the courage to act on it; and stick it out until we come into some clearing in the woods and know, intuitively, that that is where we belong.

TRAVELING THROUGH TIMES OF LOSS

Painful transitions are a natural process of our own evolving nature—as well as of the world that is changing around us. But seldom do we welcome these changes, for they pry us out of our assumptions, patterns of operation, marching plans, and expectations. Perhaps the most traumatic example of this is the loss of a partner or loved one through death, divorce, or disability, producing such an enormously unwelcome encounter with the unplanned. All of life is attachment and loss, an unavoidable, rhythmic exchange.

Any of us will suffer the weight of these iron passages in many ways. Perhaps most disconcerting is the fact that with the loss of a partner, one is now free to plan one's own journey in a wholly new way. This freedom, this privilege, has of course been bought at a high price, but it is therefore to be grasped with gratitude. Often, however, we feel a form of anger at being left with so many tasks, so many things to cover now that were perhaps handled by the partner. In those moments, we are forced to face our various dependencies, however difficult they may seem. But again, this encounter with new tasks is a freedom, an invitation to take on more than is comfortable to us. It is in these gray, tenebrific hours that we grow, become a larger person, more self-sufficient, and more capable of governing our own lives.

The word *grief* comes from the Latin *gravis*, which means "heavy," from which we get *grave* and *gravity*. Grieving is a weight upon the spirit, to be sure. Yet, the way to honor grief is to experience it fully, knowing that we grieve whatever was of value to us. The way to continue our honoring is to carry that value forward and serve it as best as we can.

On a personal front, I grieve the loss of my son a few years ago. There is not a day, scarcely an hour, that I do not think of that great loss. But it does not serve him, our relationship, or the values we had in common to not go forward with my own life. I serve him best by living our common values as well as I can and seeing people in the world around me who can also be served by the sharing of those values.

Grieving is, of course, most difficult on anniversaries and holidays, which bring back the memory of better times. (I am writing these words in the run-up to the winter holidays, a time when the loss of other is most acute. As a therapist, I am always glad to get to mid-January and the return of what Freud called "life's normal miseries.") The only real pathology is *denial*. Rejecting the feeling that rises on such occasions is the pathology, a form of spiritual dishonesty. Moving forward with our lives as best we can, in whatever venues available to us, is the best way to honor those gifts that we experienced through the ones we grieve.

Grieving is honest acknowledgment of something ending; as such, it is the natural course of all things natural, including our own lives. But as things end, there are always possibilities inherent in the moments yet to come. We would not dream of walking backward down the highway, but if we do not realize that from all loss a clearing in our life opens us up to something different, we are in effect walking backward into our future. So, we grieve the loss, and we move on, enlarged and not blocked by what has been. Only in this way does the new sprig of the spirit begin to emerge from the dark loam of our souls.

There is an ancient Buddhist parable of a woman who lost her son. Grieving, she went to the Buddha to petition for her son's return. The Buddha directed her to visit *The Sorrow Tree*, a huge tree on which was depicted the sorrows of all grieving, injured persons. She walked around and contemplated her loss amid the loss of others. When she returned to the Buddha, she humbly said, "I understand; this one is mine."

What we also do not recognize sufficiently is that this human animal is built for survival. Personally, I am sickened by those who blather on about people who have suffered greatly and that they have to find "closure." One never finds closure! The wound always bleeds! But, in time, as we have seen of life's other insolubles, we grow large enough to contain what threatened to destroy us. We are equipped for the journey. We possess the resilience of our ancestors who clung to this spinning orb, tumbling through measureless space, and we survive, rich for all that has accumulated on our journey. The hard times take their place alongside the good times. It is only when they are together that we experience the richness of this journey. Again, life is never about happiness; it is about meaning. And meaning is only found in the whole picture, not in the difficult portions edited out—as people often do in their online reports to the world. No amount of right thinking, right belief, right practice will spare us these appointments with the human condition.

We get through hard times by going *through* them, as all those before us learned along the same road. Why should we think our path should be easier than what they walked? Why would we think ourselves exempt from life's difficulties? In the *Bhagavad Gita*, we are told of two eternal birds. One is eating a fruit, and one is watching. A part of us is always engaged in the archaic bloody truth that sustaining life requires the sacrifice of some other life, and a part of us observes, gains a steadfast perspective, and understands. As my friend Stephen Dunn writes in his poem "Loves":

> Here is where loveliness can live
> with failure, and nothing's complete.
> I love how we go on.[5]

SPIRITUAL MATURITY

Getting through these most difficult in-between times requires that we gain access to a picture larger than we. If you recall Jung's comment that we all desire something larger than us, something that reframes our experience and puts it into a depth dimension, then we are obliged to develop, whether conscious or not, whether overt or not, a deeper, more mature spirituality.

Why do we say "more mature spirituality"? Does that mean "religion"? The etymology of the word *religion* (re-legare) means "to bind back to" or "to reconnect"; therefore, it is a confession of disconnection. Presumably, this reconnection is with God—or the "Ground of Being," as Tillich called it. It might also be reconnection with our own natures or our souls.

Historically, most people have assumed that the Other was wholly transcendent, and perhaps it is. But all encounters that we have are experienced inwardly, the only way we know them. So, it might be equally argued that the reconnecting might also be annealing the split-off ego complex with the rich, resonant unconscious field in which we swim all our lives. We then may be less estranged from the ground of our being and more readily supported and guided by it. This is called "healing."

Sadly, more and more people are feeling the absence of such connection in the institutions that have claimed to be its repositories for centuries. As I pointed out earlier, so great is our need for connection with something meaningful that the search goes underground and seeks its expression through a thousand surrogates: wealth, status, pleasure, sex, power, drugs, and so on. Accordingly, more and more people prefer the word *spirituality* because it is less encumbered than *religion*. Either way, either concept, the task is the same—to engage the soul with that which links it to the larger rather than the lesser.

A mature spirituality will, in my view, be characterized by some basic criteria. Among them are the following: Rather than provide us with simplistic answers, which certainly might go a long way to assuage the anxieties generated by ambiguity, one's spirituality humbly respects the mystery and confesses that *any understanding of the essential mystery of life that my poor brain and limited imagination can formulate is surely a product of my complexes or my need for "certainty."* (Wheresoever there is "certainty," there is either ignorance, delusion, willful stupidity, or service to complexes.) Only a spirituality that confesses that it knows not has a shot at growing, evolving, engaging the perils and uncertainties of the journey and of staying by our side when things get rough. The alternative encapsulation in "certainty," with its creeds, rituals, and guilt inducements, is what drives so many moderns away, even as their souls crave that connection.

A mature spirituality is one that *obliges me to grow, perhaps to go deeper into life than is comfortable* and that demands I live with grief, fear, and limitations rather than inflation.

A mature spirituality is one that respects *the principle of "resonance."* If some image or encounter resonates deeply within us, it has meaning for us. If it does not, it is not for us. We do not create resonance; resonance is the mutual hum of like to like, a re-sounding. If I like a particular food or painting or lifestyle, why should I demand you like it as well? We are different, and different things resonate for us. No matter how outnumbered, no matter how we wish to belong to any particular group, if it does not resonate for us, it is not for us. We can will our bodies to assemble with the others, but we cannot will resonance. It is, again, one of those autonomous systems within each of us that help us find our way through the world.

As he grew older, Jung recognized more and more that most people were struggling with a "religious or spiritual" issue, whatever the venue of their symptoms. In other words, what ego focuses upon, as we have seen, is not what it is about; it is where we have gotten separated from or never discovered, a value that helps us through whatever would otherwise pull us under. He also phrased it in this way: The "cure" we seek is not in resolution of a conflict but in transcendence of its debilitating opposites. The "cure" is in "the approach to the numinous"—that is, that which touches us most deeply and leads us into a radical encounter with that which is larger. Putting it in pictorial terms, I once had a client remanded to AA and therapy by a judge for her repeated drunken driving arrests. Naturally, she resisted both, but by rule of law, she attended both. After a few sessions, she told me that in listening to the metaphor of "the higher power," she asked herself, "What is *my* higher power?" What formed before her mind's eye was the shape of a bottle. "That," she thought, "that? That is too small!" At that moment, she got it. She moved willingly from her "treatment" plan, which had kept her enslaved to a larger frame of values. From that numinous encounter, her life moved onward to a better place. That is what Jung meant by the encounter with the numinous, in or outside the frame of any particular tradition.

In our understandable flights from difficulty, from suffering, we naturally seek more comfortable paths. But what if we find that it is in the most difficult, fretful precincts of suffering that real meaning is to be found? If we reach that understanding, we have an enlargement of consciousness, no longer driven by the flight from the difficult but by an embrace of the task that combines both the difficult and the meaning that makes all life, all joy possible. Rilke put it this way in his advice to that young poet:

> We know little, but that we must trust in what is difficult
> is a certainty that will never abandon us; it is good to
> be solitary, for solitude is difficult; that something is
> difficult must be one more reason to do it.[6]

In those moments, we transcend the opposites that tear us apart, the summons to and the flight from that lead us into holding those opposites in tension. As Jung pointed out, the task is to hold that tension of opposites as long as we can manage until the third appears. Again, "the third" is what that particular meeting of opposites invites as a developmental agenda. In sum, *Where am I asked to grow larger, to contain and be expanded by those opposites that now tear me apart?*

What if we find that it is in the most difficult, fretful precincts of suffering that real meaning is to be found?

Ask yourself, *Where do I have to grow into a psychology that holds those opposites and does not relapse into a regressive siding with one value or another?* For example, a person who experienced retribution for speaking back to another early in life gets the clear message that silence, evasion, and complicity will prove the path of greatest security. And then imagine the internal contretemps when that person is obliged to step into confrontation, to suffer the conflict, in order to serve a value that transcends the understandable desire for safety. British novelist Graham Greene once wrote in *The Power and the Glory* of a "whiskey priest" who hides behind his addiction and his chasuble and generally violates his professed values by his narcissism and infantility. At a critical moment, when his life is in danger, he crosses a border to give a condemned man the last rites, is captured himself, and is shot. Yet in that choice, Greene suggests, the priest rose above the dilemma to serve what the soul called him to do and, in that hour, perhaps redeemed a venal life of evasive dissolution. All of us, at some time or perhaps many times in our journeys, meet those critical dilemmas and have to suffer the opposites until the "third" shows us the path of their transcendence.

My last visit with my deceased son, Timothy, in New Mexico took us up into the Jemez Mountains, past *La Caldera*, a collapsed volcano, into rugged and beautiful boulder-strewn declivities. On that hike, we talked of what mattered. Is there a God? Does it make a difference? What does life call us to? It was the kind of conversation that rarely happens these days, given how distracted we all are. Apart from his sense of humor and his capacity to make fun of his old dad, what I most loved about him was his capacity to have this kind of conversation. After I flew back home, he sent me the following poem in which he reveals his wonderful imagination, his abiding sense of longing and irony, and his constant awareness that we all swim in some susurrus of mystery.

Naming Storms

I named my stuffed animals as a kid.
I had a whole zoo of playmates and
had friendships with Sea Captains and Pirates and
Hollywood Stars that were as meaningful and full.
I always assumed that everyone had secret treasure troves of friends
and,
as a teenager, had names for all my future loves.
We name our cars and boats
we name our pets like children
and our children, like pets, go on to name
their loves
just as I did and I assume
most do.
We name our storms,
and I find that all these naming games
are our attempts
at finding our own names
for some unnamed
God
who may not recognize us
without something
clever.

While Tim did not attend any house of worship, he would stop and talk to the observant ravens that perched and cawed in the branches along our path. He heard in the movement of the wind the soft sift of some passing spirit. He was acutely aware as a modern that he walked among the spectral presences and sacred trusts of those civilizations that had once trod the same rugged slopes. His was a deep spirituality, one that did not lend itself to modern mercantile values. His love of people was how he worshipped. His love of art was how he compromised with the claims of the monetized world of Santa Fe tourism. I bring him to this discussion to say that he intuitively understood what Jung meant that the solution to life's dilemmas is through an encounter with the numinous. For him, the tangible world was transparent, and it exuded the luminously numinous everywhere he looked. His sensibility was closer to the animistic spirits of the souls who once traversed those same slopes than to the tawdry world of politics, which he also studied and participated in, knowing that the conditions of daily life matter too. Until we can find that which links us to that which transcends us, in whatever arena we may find it, we will be torn apart by the opposites; until then, our conflicts have brought us only suffering without meaning.

It is through such respect for the deep, deep dialogue with the psyche that is commenting on our life at all times, through tracking where "the third" is to be found in our separate lives, and through caring enough to stick it out that we will be equipped to live through in-between times. Nature equipped us for the journey. Who are we to protest?

9

A Map to Meaning: What We Can Learn from Jung

Why do you wonder that travel abroad does no good, when you carry yourself along? What drove you from home still sticks close.

SOCRATES, as cited by Seneca

Of all modern thinkers, as will come as no surprise to the reader, I consider Carl Jung the person who reflected most deeply on the meaning of this short visitation we call our lives. He appreciated the timeless dimensions of our psyche, the region in which the same psychic structuring process courses through each of us, past and present. He labeled this energy field "the collective unconscious." So, you may have a dream tonight that was dreamt millennia ago by another soul, with both dreams serving both an ordering principle and a healing agenda. These organizing patterns are what he called *archetypes*.

It might be useful to think of an archetype as a verb and not a noun. If it were the latter, it would be an object and would show up in your MRI or CAT scan. Rather, as a verb, it is an organizing and compensatory energy. While your imagery might involve an automobile and your predecessor's imagery might involve an ox cart or a chariot, the generative energy is the same. An archetype is not a kind of content but a formative system, a patterning, that helps bring to the raw chaos of nature meaning, sequence, purpose, and so on. While we might label such formative patterns as if they were nouns—ascent/descent, Mother, shadow, death/rebirth—they are experiences that cluster around a certain constellation of energies. When Joseph Campbell labeled his early work *The Hero with a Thousand Faces*, he reminded us that the archetype of the hero/heroine is the personified energy that combats our twin enemies of fear and lethargy, both of which beset our lives at all times. Being the carrier of life in the face of these intimidating and regressive powers summons each of us to the "heroic," and its arenas are as varied as our lives are varied.

Part of what Jung saw in the records of the human psyche, East and West, past and present, was the archetype of the transcendent Other, sometimes named *God* or *the gods*. The faces of "God," the creeds and practices surrounding any personal or tribal experience of the transcendent "Other," will vary, will come and go; what is timeless is that large Other that we intuit as a species. For this reason, he considered religion neither an infantile regression, as Freud did, nor an opiate, as Marx did. He interpreted the data of historical record, the processes of his patients, and his own experience as an inherent desire for meaningful connection to that which is larger than we.

As we briefly saw in the preceding chapters, the erosion of tribal and institutional images that once possessed the power to link our ancestors with the transcendent energies of the cosmos has left millions of moderns reaching for secular surrogates. Jung noted that what we call "depth psychology" had to be invented toward the end of the nineteenth century to help individuals who had fallen out of the collective practices into the wasteland. While their disconnect from guiding meanings might somaticize, pathologize, or end as projections on those secular surrogates, the most common etiology was a loss of meaning, the loss of a bigger picture in which to locate one's own journey. Though he began as a psychiatrist, working in a psychiatric ward that specialized in schizophrenia and the various pathologies of the human soul, he evolved in his own understanding through and beyond the merely medical model to recognize that only when we engage the numinous in our lives can we reframe our suffering and find its meaning.

Although we are never free of suffering or conflict or loss, we are invited to grow larger than the fearful cost each inflicts upon us. Easy issues are solved through behavioral and attitudinal changes; we all know that. But few of us know or want to recognize that the core issues of life are never solved. At best, we can outlive some of the lesser resolutions we brought to them. Accordingly, any understanding I gain today will necessarily need revisioning by what life will bring me tomorrow. I saw a cartoon years ago in which a therapist said to the client, "I cannot solve your problem, but I can give you a more compelling story for your misery."

I have more than once said to clients that what we hoped to achieve together was an enlargement that comes from taking life on, from leaving behind lesser road maps and stratagems, and, in the end, having a more interesting life. When we are young, we may fantasize that we can figure out the "answers" to life's dilemmas. As we mature and suffer slowly into wisdom, we learn that whatever those "answers" were, they prove insufficient for the experiences to follow. Achieving a steadfastness in the face of the changing topography of our lives, the courage to address what must be addressed, and the willingness to go back to the drawing board occasionally are what provide us an alternative to superficiality and sentimentality, as well as to their cousins, cynicism and bitterness.

In the following pages and topics, I ask you to absorb these few of Jung's many profound observations and consider how they might help you find meaning in the conduct of your daily, ever-changing life.

THE REAL ISSUES OF LIFE ARE NEVER SOLVED, BUT THEY MAY BE OUTGROWN

It is the natural desire and tendency of conscious life to solve problems and then move on. This proclivity does indeed lead to the resolution of many, if not most, of life's dilemmas—but not of the ones that matter most.

Jung himself shared our desire for quick and happy resolution to the conflicts and stuck places. As he describes,

> I had always worked with the temperamental conviction that at bottom there are no insoluble problems, and experience justified me in so far as I have often seen patients simply outgrow a problem that had destroyed others. This "outgrowing," as I formerly called it, proves on further investigation to be a new level of consciousness. Some higher or wider interest appeared on the patient's horizon, and through this broadening of outlook the insoluble problem lost its urgency. It is not solved logically in its own terms, but faded out when confronted with a new and stronger life urge.[1]

How often the old adage "sleep on it" brings a measure of relief the next day when we have been able to step out of the emotional morass and reframe it in some way. Our unconscious has also worked on it to provide a new perspective. Notable artistic and scientific discoveries have risen out of this outer/inner world dialectic. Clearly, some autonomous energy within us continues to work on a problem and often comes up with perspectives, even avenues of resolution, unknown to conscious life.

Still, many of life's issues are not solvable. For example, sometimes quanta of trauma remain in our system and send up bubbles to trouble our days, just as a sunken ocean liner releases its flotsam for decades. (The USS *Arizona* is still leaking oil at Pearl Harbor after nearly eighty years.) Sometimes betrayals, profound losses, roads not taken continue to haunt us and cloud the present. We will never "solve" these experiences for they are always part of our psychoactive history. But consciously, we can attend to the business of living in the present. Asking the question, *What does this old, persisting problem make me do or keep me from doing?*, obliges us to take responsibility for what spills into the world through us.

Some years ago, in a book called *Swamplands of the Soul*, I suggested that our periodic visitations to dismal places—depression, loss, betrayal, grief, and so on—were part of the human condition from which none of us is exempt. But to move beyond a posture of outrage at life's "betrayal," we are called to ask another question: *To what present task is this swampland calling me?* Asking this question moves us from a posture of victimhood to engagement with the unfolding of our destiny. Without this move, fate triumphs over destiny.

Jung summarizes, "The greatest and most important problems of life are fundamentally insoluble. They must be so, for they express the necessary polarity inherent in every self-regulating system. They can never be solved, but only outgrown."[2] In this observation, Jung reminds us that when we lean to one side of any equation, any dilemma, we create an imbalance that sooner or later will need recompense. In analytic psychology, the opposite of any truth is always, also, true. The ego consciousness is dismayed by this fact but is obliged to enlarge to deal with it. Similarly, the ultimate gift of relationship is not that we find someone to take care of us (that person is already on the scene—us) or to spare us our appointments with destiny but rather to bring us their "otherness." Engaging their otherness obliges our enlargement, sometimes painfully so. Living with ambiguity, not being too attached to the old "certainties," and learning what life needs to tell us whether or not we think we are up to it are, frankly, the only ways we grow, become more capacious, live a larger journey. Meanwhile, the task of living goes onward, with or without our participation. It is up to us to foster that broader outlook that catalyzes growth.

THE CURE FOR LONELINESS IS SOLITUDE

Even when we are surrounded by people, we are alone: alone with our bodies, alone with our spirits, our fears, and our individualized summons to step into our journeys. There was a rush of expectation with the vast transformation of our society by social media and by the internet itself. To be sure, we have greater access to each other now, we can find each other more easily, but we can also annoy each other more incessantly, intrude more abruptly, and use and abuse each other more profoundly by bombarding folks with unwanted commercial, religious, political, sentimentalized, and trivial chaff.

(Wherever the human imprint advances, the Shadow follows apace.) For all the connectivity the modern electronic world offers, and I do appreciate that gift, I also perceive that we are more atomized, more disconnected from each other than ever before.

When Freud was still living in Vienna, he got a letter from his daughter in London and spoke to a colleague about it: "Imagine the modern world. I got this letter in only three days. But if it were not the modern world, I could walk in the other room and talk to her." While we all applaud modern freedom of movement, as well as social and psychological latitude whereby most of us no longer live with our tribe, we seem further and further separated from each other and what matters most to us. And yet, most of us cannot name a real "tribe" to which we belong at all.

Loneliness can catalyze as a disease or a blessing, depending on the psychology we bring to it. The flight from aloneness can also be seen as a flight from ourselves. Where we were once connected to the heartbeat of the universe, with all needs met, we were abruptly, traumatically flung at birth into primal separation, not unlike an astronaut space-walker whose tether breaks and drifts off and away from the "mother ship." One can imagine that much of life is trying to merge again with that primal Other, seeking to feel safe, protected, and nurtured. There is nothing wrong with those needs, of course, but when they prevail, the "treatment plan" often sabotages our growing up, undermines that which we are meant to bring into the world as individuating souls. For example, such an urge to merge keeps people in terrible relationships because they fear being alone, or it keeps them from standing for their values for fear of rejection. While these fears are natural and common, they also represent an abrogation of our summons to become ourselves more fully.

Even when we think we are set and secure, life can tear that other away through death, divorce, disability, or choice. Attachment is always attached to loss. Moreover, we could make the case that perfect parenting is characterized by having offered first reassurances and then progressive "abandonment," titrated to fit the child's increasing capacity to manage for his- or herself. Just as abandonment creates lifelong insecurities, so clinging to a child, hovering, creates dependencies and sends the silent message: "You can't manage this life on your own; you always need me to help." The generation produced by contemporary "helicopter parents" will not fare well in the real world that awaits them.

A former colleague once said she could usually tell in the first hour or so whether the patient was "a big kid, or a little kid." The former could do the work of growing up, and the latter was still looking for the surrogate "parent" to manage their life. Similarly, I have seen that a prognosis depends largely on the capacity of the person to take responsibility for his or her life, to cease blaming, or to cease looking for rescue from someone. Psychologist Clark Moustakas concluded, "Efforts to overcome the existential experience of loneliness can result only in self-alienation. When [one] successfully evades and denies the terrible loneliness of individual existence, he shuts himself off from the one significant avenue of his own self-growth."[3] Clearly, that aloneness requires that we begin to develop greater self-awareness and coping skills, confront dependencies that hid out in the old relationships, and find new, unexplored rooms in our psychic mansion. Anton Chekhov once wryly observed, "If you are afraid of loneliness, don't marry." His observation was reinforced by Rilke's short lyric "*Einsamkeit*," or "Loneliness." After a couple has made love, he notes their *postcoital triste* and observes that the river of loneliness still flows onward between them. Why should it be *triste*? Perhaps, because after the *conjunction* comes the return to one's own lone being.

While friends, partners, and associations with others can be supportive, challenging, and dialectically developmental, it is also true that we grow most when we are on our own, when we have to figure out our path, when we have to find the courage to live it. Staying plugged in, merging with others, surrounding ourselves with noise of all kinds—all are flights from being with ourselves. And yet, the only cure for loneliness is solitude. When we achieve solitude, we are not alone when we are alone. We are present to ourselves, and we have an earnest dialogue transpiring with that Other who is also us.

Jung put it best when he wrote,

> The highest and most decisive experience of all . . .
> is to be alone with . . . [one's] own self, or whatever
> else one chooses to call the objectivity of the
> psyche. The patient must be alone if he is to find out
> *what it is that supports him when he can no longer
> support himself.* Only this experience can give him an
> indestructible foundation. (emphasis added)[4]

Another way to phrase that may be that we need to find what supports us when nothing supports us—that is, when the experience of the loss of the other is upon us and we are flush with separation anxiety, rather than run to the nearest safe harbor, we sit with it and sit it out. During that time, we learn, often to our surprise, that something rises within to support us. We will not perish, though we think we will. By bearing the unbearable, we go through the desert to arrive at a nurturing oasis we did not know was there.

We need to find what supports us when nothing supports us. By bearing the unbearable, we go through the desert to arrive at a nurturing oasis we did not know was there.

How wonderful it is to know that one has that resilient strength within. Recently, in a conversation with my analyst friend and colleague, Jan Bauer of Montreal, she reminded me of how isolated and depressed we were in our Zurich days of analytic training, living away from friends and family, in a foreign culture and with a foreign language. She recalled that our analysts didn't tell us ten easy steps to get out of the depression; they told us to go back to our shabby rooms and sit with it until its meaning emerged for us. Some did, and some didn't. Those who did came out with a stronger sense of their souls and of what supported them when nothing supported them.

The antidote to loneliness is letting go of the fantasy that the attachment to the Other is necessary to our survival. (Certainly, the essence of pop music and media is that the Other is necessary for one's survival, the loss of whom is catastrophic.) The antidote is to know that there is no antidote to be found, ultimately, and that that is okay. After all, most relationships fail because we ask too much of them. Is it not possible that more might survive if we asked less of them and more of ourselves? This is why Rilke defined a healthy relationship as a person being the guardian of the solitude of the Other. No matter how much we care or are cared for, we cannot live the other's life or spare them difficulty, nor can they spare us. What remains after the delusions are gone can be pretty wonderful. As Jung concluded, "Loneliness is not inimical to companionship, for no one is more sensitive to companionship than the lonely man, and companionship thrives only when each individual remembers his individuality."[5] So, it seems, solitude is an achievement, an aloneness that is not loneliness and that is not dependent on another to rescue us. Far from the narcissist's need for constant reassurance, solitude is the self-care system doing its proper job. It means we can tolerate being with ourselves, and if that is the case, then perhaps others will be able to tolerate being with us also.

OUR BEST, MOST DEMANDING, AND MOST USEFUL JOB IS ADDRESSING OUR OWN SHADOWS

The world has never lacked for idealists. I am a recovering idealist myself. Of course, I still have ideals, but I have seen enough of the world now that I do not expect to see them realized, even though a good part of the value of my life is pursuing them nonetheless. The world has never lacked for utopian schemes, noble institutions, and people of the highest intentions. And yet, something always goes wrong. Putting it simply: no matter how noble or well-intended we or our institutions are, we always mess things up, sooner or later. This perspective is not pessimistic; it is simply a factual observation of the whole bloody train of history. As Jung put it in his critique of what we, with all our scientific and technological advancements, have been able to accomplish:

> Man has been delivered from no fear, a hideous
> nightmare lies upon the world. So far reason has
> failed lamentably, and the very thing that everyone
> wanted to avoid rolls on in ghastly progression. Man

> has achieved a wealth of useful gadgets, but, to
> offset that, he has torn open the abyss, and what will
> become of him now—where can he make a halt?[6]

He knows where to place the blame for all this self-destructive behavior: on you and me. As he noted further, "Man's worst sin is unconsciousness, but it is indulged in with the greatest piety even by those who serve mankind as teachers and examples."[7] Well, that certainly gives us an assignment. We all assume that learning, rationality, and good intentions will prove enough to bring us to the Promised Land; but they haven't, and they won't. The reason for this is that we also are creatures of swarming agendas, disparate clusters of autonomous, split-off energies, and we always have a considerable capacity for self-delusion. Jung's notion of the Shadow is most helpful to us to consider our assignment more deeply.

The Shadow represents those elements, energies, and agendas in us or in our affiliative associations that, when brought to consciousness, contradict our professed values. The Shadow is not evil, per se, though much evil derives from it; rather, the Shadow embodies the contrarian dimensions of our souls. Put most succinctly, what is wrong in the world is wrong in us as well. As the Latin playwright Terence wrote over two millennia ago, "Nothing human is alien to me." So, the work of improving the world begins in my own backyard.

The Shadow manifests in four interactive fields. First, it is most commonly unconscious and therefore spills into the world, into our relationships, onto our children unconsciously. We only become aware of Shadow infiltrations when we have to start dealing with their consequences. Second, we can disown our Shadow by seeing it in others—the person I blame, the people across that geophysical border, those with a different religion or pigmentation or cultural form. All of bigotry, prejudice, and war comes from such projection. Third, I can become possessed by the Shadow and swept along by its powerful energy. We can revel in our violence, our dangerous habits and behaviors. We can flaunt the norms like adolescents and smile while doing it. Last, we can become conscious of our Shadow; that is when the real work begins. As Stephen Dunn ruefully concluded, "The good news is I know who I am; that's the bad news too."[8]

In 1937, while speaking at Yale, Jung spoke of what happens to a person who takes on the Shadow. Such a person, he says,

> has become a serious problem to himself, as he is now unable to say that *they* do this or that, *they* are wrong, and *they* must be fought against. . . . Such a man knows that what is wrong in the world is in himself, and if he only learns to deal with his own shadow he has done something real for the world. He has succeeded in shouldering at least an infinitesimal part of the gigantic, unsolved social problems of our day. . . . How can anyone see straight when he does not even see himself and the darkness he unconsciously carries with him into all his dealings.[9]

Admittedly, it is very hard to consider oneself the chief source of one's problems. All of us have been hurt, and hurt badly, by life. That is a given. But what rises out of that is, of course, our "story" about that hurt. And then the pragmatic questions remain: *What does that story make me do or keep me from doing?* Shadow work involves examining our virtues and the opposite of our virtues, for they, too, are entering the world through us, though we may not know it without some sincere, humbling examination. *Where does my jealousy assert itself? Where does my anger leak out? Where does my guilt push me down some long alley?* These questions are inherently humbling, and no one likes being humbled or having to admit culpability, but until we do so, our unaddressed life keeps entering the world. While a shadowless person is either an unconscious or a superficial person, dealing with our Shadow is the only way we can bring a bit more freedom to those around us—our children, partners, neighbors, fellow citizens. What I am unwilling to face in myself will always be carried by someone else. Perhaps we are only here to help each other get through life. Unburdening our partners, children, neighbors by lifting our stuff off of them is one way to start.

OUR PSYCHE WISHES TO BE HEARD

Perhaps the most accessible way to understand our many distresses, both personal and societal, is to consider wherever we are aligned against nature. While thoughtful people know that we cannot continue to plunder our planet without nature reacting violently—and we have much evidence of that happening already—as a culture, we blithely continue lives of waste, exploitation, and valorizing profit as the primary metric for cultural success. Nature's response will not be pretty.

So, too, whenever we stop growing, enquiring, exploring, our psyche pathologizes as depression, or we self-medicate or look for ever-new ways to divert ourselves. While we continue to walk, employing Jung's metaphor, in shoes too small for ourselves, captive to both our external pressures and our phenomenological "stories" of adaptation, we are mostly unprepared to undertake the second half of life. As Jung noted, "We have no schools for forty-year-olds. . . . Our religions were always such schools in the past, but how many people regard them like that today?"[10]

When I left academia thirty years ago, I was not leaving education; I was leaving conversations with adolescents for conversations with adults who, by forty and older, had both achieved enough ego strength to reflect on their journey with all its problems and achieved a history that demands such reflection. My investment in this second-half-of-life educational project has led me to work with and for various Jung societies around the world, as well as to write books the chief purpose of which is to bridge the gap between the sometimes arcane thought of Jung and a public that has so much to gain from his insights.[11]

The ancient ones had their sacred stories and rituals that linked our ancestors to the various orders of mystery, the whirling cosmos, the world of nature of which they were a part, the participation in tribal life, and the conduct of a purpose-filled journey. As those linking images, stories, and rituals have waned in their efficacy, they have left us to our own devices. And yet, each of us has our own *daimon*. A *daimon* is an inspirited, bridging entity that visits the in-between of gods and humans. Socrates professed that he, as ego consciousness, did not philosophize but that the *daimon* spoke through his ego structure into the world. Similarly, Plato considered that the *daimon*, also known as the *muse*, possesses the artist and uses the painter or musician as a vehicle of expression. I have experienced, and no doubt the reader has also, the many times when I was working on a problem or living through a difficult decision, and suddenly the path for me became clear. When young and no one else was in the room with me, I might have claimed that I had figured it out on my own; I did not have any idea of what was really working within and through me.

Accordingly, the single biggest, most compelling area of investigation for me is what I see of this autonomous Other working through my analytic clients and through myself. Something is always trying to work its way through us into the world. Growing and developing require being open to that encounter, surrendering to it, and serving the exfoliation of meaning it brings to us. Jung put it very forcefully: "Deviation from the truths of the blood begets neurotic restlessness, and we have had about enough of that these days. Restlessness begets meaninglessness, and the lack of meaning in life is a soul-sickness whose full extent and full import our age has not yet begun to comprehend."[12]

Our *daimon* is our tutelary and constant companion. It has been there from childhood to the present, but it is usually drowned out by the noise of our environment, the fears that haunt us, the "stories" that separate us, and the sundry distractions popular culture offers to help us avoid our own souls. Put simply, our *daimon* is our personal link to wisdom, to that which transcends ordinary ego consciousness. It embodies what is right for us, no matter how trying that summons will prove to the comfort motives of the ego.

Something is always trying to work its way through us into the world. Our nature is forever changing and seeking growth.

History is replete with those we admire for submitting their ego's agendas before the summons of the *daimon*. Large souls like Nelson Mandela, Martin Luther King Jr., and Dietrich Bonhoeffer surely wished normal lives like ours, but their souls demanded they sacrifice the normal desire for comfort, for safety, and for fitting in to respond to the injustices of their time. Our nature is forever changing and seeking growth; when outer forces or inner resistance oppose that growth, we experience a terrible deadening of the spirit. So many humans still suffer this diminution of spirit by the social constructs that limit them, or by fear-ridden "stories," whose adaptive strategies take them further and further from their possible appointment with destiny. Just think of the constrictive role gender definitions and proscriptions play in damaging souls or of how so many people get estranged from their bodies and healthy sexuality. So much suffering has arisen for individuals out of the codification of group fears in normative "oughts" and "shoulds." Wherever nature's voice is constricted, the Shadow goes underground and works its way into the branching paths of pathology.

The growth of the psyche may take its form in learning new things, in travel and exploration in many forms, or simply in sitting with ourselves and listening to our souls from time to time. In his poem "Homecoming," German poet Friedrich Hölderlin wrote, "That which thou seeketh is near, and already coming to meet thee." Imagine that—the possibility of knowing what is right for us is so close at hand all the while. And then, of course, we have to find the courage to live it.

FEAR AND LETHARGY ARE OUR GREATEST OPPONENTS

In 1912, Jung published a revolutionary and difficult book, now revised and retitled *Symbols of Transformation*. While he recognized the directive role our instincts play, as did Freud, and how we are socialized, as did Alfred Adler, he also asserted that the human animal possesses a "symbolic life"—that is, an awareness that there is a field of invisible energies at work within our lives and that we are creatures of the spirit, as well as bodies and relational associations. This work ostensibly analyzes the active imagination text of a woman he never met, passed on to him by a colleague. In it, Jung explores the spontaneous psychomythic dynamics of the symbol-making animal.

In her active imagination text, the writer embodies a hero-lover figure through the persona of an Aztec chieftain. In reflecting on the archetypal gestalt of the hero, Jung notes how each of us has an innate cluster of energy whose task it is to overthrow the dark powers that threaten, whether outer or inner. The outer threats are the powers and principalities of this earth that confront us and generate fear. In the face of fear, he notes, "the spirit of evil is fear, negation, the adversary who opposes life in its struggle for eternal duration and thwarts every great deed."[13] Each of us knows this well, for more of our reflexive, patterning behaviors arise out of fear management, or rather our being managed by fear, than out of any other motive. And yet, each of us also knows a summons to show up in life as ourselves, no matter how deeply buried that impulse is. Jung continues, "For the hero, fear is a challenge and task, because only boldness can deliver from fear. And if the risk is not taken, the meaning of life is somehow violated, and the whole future is condemned to a hopeless staleness, to a drab grey lit only by will-o'-the-wisps."

As intimidating as the outer world can be, there is a far greater, far more insidious force within us that can equally sabotage the project our journey seeks to bring into the world. That force is found in the seduction of unconsciousness, indolence, which Jung labeled as our greatest vice. Speaking of the hero, Jung writes, "Always he imagines his worst enemy in front of him, yet carries the enemy within himself—a deadly longing for the abyss, a longing to drown in his own source." Recognized by our ancestors as well, "this regressive tendency has been consistently opposed from the most primitive times by the great psychotherapeutic systems which we know as the religions. They seek to create an autonomous consciousness by weaning mankind away from the sleep of childhood." Jung is suggesting here that the rites of passage and doctrinal allegiances of religion mobilize the human libido into forms of action that preserve and empower the survival of the tribe and the individual, thus preventing a regression into dependencies and sloth.

We all have this titanic struggle going on within each of us every day. The ego, whipsawed between fear and lethargy, can easily be intimidated or seduced to the point that our life never happens. It is no crime to have fear; that is human. It is, however, a crime to only lead a fearful life. Many think courage is being fearless, but only the psychotic or delusional are fearless. Courage is showing up in the face of the large world and its powers. And the power of lethargy must not be forgotten either, especially in a society such as ours, with its ready access to soporific chemicals that numb us and fantasies that distract us. After all, we live in a culture that whispers in our ear, "When the going gets tough, the tough go shopping."

All of us are the humble carriers of the spark of life and the project of individuation. Individuation does not mean a fatuous, narcissistic self-absorption but rather a submission to what wants to enter the world through us. Life is not here to serve us; we are here to serve life. This means that we have to face these outer and inner obstacles, fear and lethargy, every day. Each of us; no one is exempt.

Life is not here to serve us; we are here to serve life.

I live in a four-story condominium, and every morning, I take an elevator down six stories into the underground level where my car sits. As the elevator descends, I say to myself these simple six words. You can borrow them if you wish or get your own mantra.

Shut up.
Suit up.
Show up.

The first tells me to stop whining and complaining. Most of us live privileged lives. Most—not all—of us have food on the table, a roof over our head, and relative security of person. So, stop complaining; simply shut up. The second tells me to work at what is worthy of my commitment. Get prepared. Do the homework. No excuses for not being ready to take on what the day brings us.

The last tells me that we all have to show up—that is, just do our best. Throw ourselves into it. No one is perfect; no one is ever finished; no one ever gets out of this life alive. Just do it as well as you can. That is all anyone can ask; that is all that history asks. Try to forgive yourself from time to time along the way. Life is here to be served. It is all a blooming mystery, and we will never figure it out. (And don't pay any attention to any of those palookas who tell you they have.) But one thing is clear: we are here to bring our selves, our best selves, to this troubled orb plunging through oceans of space.

We are often gripped by fear, by the comforting powers of the old adaptations whose chief virtues were anxiety management and protection. Or, alternatively, our path ahead is blocked by familiar apprehensions about stepping into the unknown on our own. No wonder we tend to abide the familiar, stultifying as it may be. Yet something within us always knows, always protests, always begins to withdraw approval and support even as we ratify our old inner divisions and archaic stories.

Ego consciousness, tasked with making it all work, labors to satisfy the Anxiety Party clamoring in the back benches of the inner Parliament for surcease, for return to the old order. The insurgent Soul Party agitates for growth, renewal, risk, and enlargement, and the Honorable Ego Prime Minister is beset with the impossible task of keeping these belligerents happy. No wonder this shaky government is overthrown each night by troubling dreams filled with brigands and guerillas stirring revolt in the provinces. No wonder so many resign this struggle for personal authority and consign their value choices to directive traditions, to external leaders, to others, thinking it easier to get along by going along. If only those internal brigands and guerillas would cooperate, it would all work out. But every night, in slumber's sugar canebrakes, they agitate anew, and the insurrection within bubbles. And sooner or later, they march on the Capitol.

So, how can we find our way, make the right choices? Sometimes we just can't, and we have to live in the midst of the very uncomfortable for a very long time, until something unexpected appears from within. As Jung writes,

> You can only feel yourself on the right road when the conflicts of duty seem to have resolved themselves, and you have become the victim of a decision made over your head or in defiance of the heart. From this we can see the numinous power of the Self, which can hardly be experienced in any other way. For this reason, the experience of the Self is always a defeat for the ego.[14]

In other words, the ultimate decisions of our lives are made by some higher agency than the ego. Ego intentionality is tasked with the governance of daily life. But when ego consciousness can accord itself with the will of the Self, there is a profound sense of the rightness, the peace, the accord that comes from a moment of wholeness when we are at one with ourselves, and not this split, divided, warring assemblage of fractious parties.

WE ARE THE MEANING-MAKERS

Jean-Paul Sartre spoke of our desire for a reliable road map, a dependable guide to life's querulous choices: "There is no traced out path to lead man to his salvation; he must constantly invent his own path. But, to invent it he is free, responsible, without excuse, and every hope lies within him."[15] Quite naturally, we would all like a road map: clear instructions, great teachers, and the sanction of the collective approval. And, of course, we can learn from others and from great literature, as we learned from brother Hamlet's contretemps. But to take someone else's path, no matter how sincerely, is to be living someone else's journey, and not our own. We may think we have nothing to bring to the table, no chip to add to the great mosaic, but that is how we wind up undermining our summons to personhood. The reader will recall Jung's reminder that sometimes one simply has to be "alone if [we are] to find out what it is that supports [us] when [we] no longer can support ourselves. Only this experience can give [us] an indestructible foundation."[16]

Jung challenges us to consider that within each of us is a center that is wiser than our knowledge, deeper than our learning, older than our chronology, and more durable than our calcified convictions. From time to time, life humbles us, calls us to account, leads us back to the drawing board, and asks us to start over. Isn't it nice to think there might also be some resources available there to help us when we think we are bereft, when we have exhausted our conscious tools, when we have lost our way?

In writing about the aims of psychotherapy in 1929, Jung observed that the therapeutic project is less about "cure," for life is not a disease, and more about an ongoing experiment to be lived through. So, the common work, he asserts, "is less a question of treatment than of developing the creative possibilities latent within the patient."[17]

As projects of nature, we are infinitely adaptable, resilient, and resourceful. Without these attributes, this animal species we are would not have been able to survive the perils of this planet. Just as we adapt to the various powers around us—adaptations that often distort, even violate our own souls—so we manage to wedge ourselves into the narrow slots where external forces so often maneuver us. While these adaptations allow us to fit into our family structures or social environments, they also tend to cost us a great deal. Every adaptation, however obliged by outer pressures, risks a further injury to the psyche that will not go unaddressed by the soul. So, bombarded as we are by the cacophonous claims of contemporary culture, we find ways to fit in; and the hidden cost of doing so shows up in our disturbing dreams, our anesthetizing addictions, or our sundry forms of denial or distraction. How many of us, for example, have tried to do "the right thing," as defined by our family messages, our cultural imperatives and prohibitions, or by succumbing to the pressures of the hour, and then felt empty within, used, exploited, betrayed somehow? The perverse irony is that these same adaptations that often allow us to "fit in" become traps, constraints that also contain or deform the developmental desires that course through us.

When we understand psychopathology as the quite legitimate protest of the psyche, as a summons to take seriously a wider range of life's choices, we realize that we do have an internal guidance system. If I am doing all "the right things," why is it I have to keep forcing the energy, fighting off the doubts and depressions, and keep trying to stay ahead of whatever is pursuing me? Jung speaks to this common phenomenon quite clearly and powerfully. He notes that so many of his cases "are not suffering from any clinically definable neurosis, but from the senselessness and aimlessness of their lives. I should not object if this were called the general neurosis of our age."

Most of us really "know" what is right for us, though we may be frightened or intimidated to know what we already know. As Jung put it, "Most of my patients knew the deeper truth, but did not live it.

And why did they not live it? Because of that bias which makes us all live from the ego, a bias which comes from overvaluation of the conscious mind." By "conscious mind," Jung essentially means the mind that is occupied by the complex triggered in that moment. So, seldom are we "in our right mind"; most of the time, we are subsumed by and serving the invisible text of a "message," which means we serve the received authority rather than our own deepest promptings.

So much of the self-help genre prattles on about "happiness." "Thirty Days to This or That," "Five Easy Steps to (fill in the blank)." But this pablum does not feed the soul, fire the spirit, create the new world. The pursuit of "happiness" is seductive but delusory. Happiness is a by-product of those rare moments of détente, of concordance between our external choices and our internal reality. As Jung writes in another essay, "The principle aim of psychotherapy is not to transport the patient to an impossible state of happiness but to help him acquire steadfastness and philosophic patience in the face of suffering. Life demands for its completion and fulfillment a balance between joy and sorrow."

In the end, we prove to be more than just social animals; we are meaning-seeking, meaning-creating creatures. As Jung notes, "The least of things with a meaning is always worth more in life than the greatest of things without it."

FROM WHENCE COMETH, AND WHITHER TO?

We spend so much of daily life in meeting obligations, in serving schedules, assignments, and legitimate obligations, most of which are important and life serving. But the by-product of this immersion in the topography of our time is the loss of that second bird's observational perspective, the large view, the synoptic vision. Put simply, *What is our life all about? Why are we even here? What are we to do while being here?*

My several clients who are seventy-plus find that so many of their dreams are reviewing their life history, revealing some of the stuck points, and, occasionally, lifting out of the tide of history the patterning force that created those waves, those ebbs and flows we call our biographies. Thanks to dreamwork and other conversations, many of them have discerned patterns in themselves. While it is easiest to discern the patterns generated by complexes, the avoidances, the compliances, the subtle trade-offs with anxiety, it is much harder to discern the patterns that intimate an invisible force that is moving and shaping us. (However often quoted, I cannot help but remind us of brother Hamlet's words, "There is a destiny that shapes our ends . . . rough hew them as we will.") And so there is a "destiny," that which seeks expression through us, unfolding in such large, sometimes gentle, sometimes turbulent waves that we have difficulty seeing their shaping contours. But they are there, and it is important, if we are privileged to live long enough, to be able to look at them and respect that some force far greater than our conscious intentions, far greater than the powers of our environmental influences, has been at work all the while.

I suspect that similar thoughts were on his mind when the octogenarian Carl Jung, having received repeated requests, dictated his memoir *Memories, Dreams, Reflections*. He informs the reader early on that the book is not an autobiography of his outer life, despite references to Freud and his many travels; rather, it is a tracking of the way in which his inner life grew, developed, unfolded. If anyone had the right to make final judgments about life and what is worth affirming, Jung had that right. But with great humility he demurs, steps aside, and says that he has no general conclusions to offer, no advice, no grand philosophy. Instead, as he looks at his journey, he is most moved by the unfolding patterns.

> I have no judgement about myself and my life. There is nothing I am quite sure about. I have no definite convictions—not about anything, really. I know only that I was born and exist, and it seems to me that I have been carried along. I exist on the foundation of something I do not know. In spite of all uncertainties, I feel a solidity underlying all existence and a continuity in my mode of being.[18]

These are remarkable words and remarkably humble words. No convictions, no certainties, despite a lifetime, a rich lifetime, of inquiry and massive research, and yet no conscious picture of the engine coordinating all these moving parts. And still, a deep, abiding connection, a solidity, a continuity unfolding through him. Would that we all might feel that deep sense of participation in the mystery and wonder of being here. Then we would be living what Jung called "the symbolic life"—a life not guided by the outer points of reference (achievements, relationships, children, status, wealth, resumes, whatever) but by a relationship to the larger questions of "being here."[19]

I, too, realize how I have been guided all these years. We are all too close to it to see it in the hectic years; but later, when we see the long wave patterns forming like an ocean liner long past but whose passage we sense in the swells that rise up on our shores, we realize the presence of an invisible source that was there all along. Many will personify this presence as the unfolding will of God; others will point to our multiple socializing influences, which do play a role; others will ascribe it to our genetic codes; and still others, to random concatenations of molecules. Perhaps we might better simply call the archetypal combination of all these forces "the gods." This is not a metaphysical or theological statement; it is a measure of respect for the autonomy of the mystery and the desire to stand somehow, in our limited human condition, in relationship to it.

When Jung said that neuroses were offended or neglected gods, he acknowledged the omnipotence of those invisible presences. The only question is this: Which metaphor best speaks to your sensibility? God, "the gods," randomness, genetics, sociopolitical constructs, whatever? When you are drawn to one metaphor or another, please remember, the symbol is not the "Thing." It simply reminds us to remember that the "Thing" is not the "Thing" and that the "Thing" is, and remains always, unknown.[20] Only then can we respect the limits of both our poor apparatus and our limited pictorial capacity. Still, we must also remember our inherent drive to know, to ponder, to suffer these things. That is what makes us humans, not doorknobs.

Sometimes our world drops away, disintegrates, suddenly appears altered in unknowable ways. We may be cast adrift in the sea of transience and uncertainty. Change is the nature of nature, and we are a part of nature. Change is how life renews; but ego consciousness seldom welcomes change because change undermines our fantasy of sovereignty, understanding, and control. The more we try to control, as those who suffer obsessive-compulsive disorders know intimately, the more life slips out of our control. The past several decades have been moments of vast social change, a deconstruction of old "verities," new barbarisms, new palliatives, new charlatans, new broken promises. What, then, keeps constancy in our souls? As Goethe asked, "*Was dauert im Wechseln?*" What abides amid change?

Change is the nature of nature, and we are a part of nature.

In a world of unpredictable, uncontrollable change, only our relationship to our guiding instincts, only our internal compass, only our dialogue with our dreams and revelatory systems of response provide continuity. Any one of us who has a relationship to our inner life, our autonomous, supportive psyche, will ride the currents of social change, as well as of personal change, and emerge on the other side.

The venerable Basho once wrote that we are all "going home." So we are, and while doing that, there are many journeys that take us away from home and ultimately lead us to a home rather different than the one we had imagined or planned for ourselves. We all have to wonder who, or what, is steering the ship? Are we the captains or the passengers? From whence we departed is now shrouded in mystery, and whither bound even more so. But it is a helluva journey, and it is *our* journey. So let us try to stay awake and look for the new shore amid the scudding mist as we navigate the sea-wracked shoals and rocky littoral that lie before us.

AFTERWORD: HOMECOMING

The meaning of my existence is that life has addressed
a question to me. Or conversely, I myself am a
question which is addressed to the world, and I must
communicate my answer, for otherwise I am dependent
upon the world's answer.

C. G. Jung

I f you have understood the thread running throughout this book, you know by now that it leads back through the thousand outer distractions and the Ariadnean maze within, to you. Remember, as Hölderlin wrote in "Homecoming," "That which thou seekest is near, and already coming to meet thee." All healing is a form of homecoming, a return to our body's wisdom, the psyche's developmental intentions, to the place linking both our origins and our destinies. But what is home, and where is it? And are we meant to stay there if we find it?

Let me tell you a true story, one I printed years ago but that bears repeating. My wife and I used to live near Atlantic City, New Jersey. While we usually disdained the tawdry, crass world of the casinos, we once accepted someone's gift of a free dinner and show. We forgot that the prophets of old said, in many variations, "There is no such thing as a free meal, even a casino meal." Like the long line of those duped before us, we went. It turned out to be a variety show with singers, comedians, magicians, and the like. And then two acrobats from Mexico asked for a volunteer from the audience. Naturally, no sane person volunteered. So, they went into the audience and dragged some "innocent" (?) stooge onto the stage. Suddenly, I found myself facing an audience of perhaps six hundred strangers.

As I recall, I wasn't nervous. Rather, it all felt surreal, dreamlike. When asked my name, I told them. When asked, "Where is your home?" I inexplicably paused, seconds passing on a live mic, like your worst nightmare from kindergarten. I remember thinking, "Now that is an interesting question. *Home*. Home? Where is my home?" Meanwhile, the audience began laughing at the dunce on stage, and the acrobats started thinking they should have grabbed the lady in the third row. After watching an internal teleprompter roll of places I had lived, I started to reply: "Zurich." But "No," I thought, "that is a metaphor, not where I reside." And so one of the acrobats said, "Asked you too tough a question?" After which, I recovered my wits and replied, "Linwood, New Jersey." Then the act followed, and while I nearly got killed in their exertions on behalf of entertaining the crowd, the truly notable event of the evening was what happened during those agonizing seconds on stage.

Upon reflection, I don't think it was nervousness or stage fright. I think the surreality of the moment caused my psyche to dissociate into two compartments. One had the literal answer to their questions; one reflected on the gravity of their question. What is home, then? When I subsequently reflected on my "answer" to their question, an answer that even in that querulous moment I knew to be symbolic and not what they were seeking, something profound revealed itself to me. I realized that home was not a place but a journey, a process. Zurich was, for me, the place of a midlife passage, a dark descent into the unexplored regions of the psyche, a time of testing of resilience and living with ambiguity over a very long period. Moreover, it was, in fact, a symbolic exile and a loss of the known world, a descent into the underworld, and then a slow recovery of a relationship to the soul once again. "Zurich" was not a city but a way station on the soul's journey. Just as some say "all roads lead to Rome" or "next year in Jerusalem" or undertake the Hajj to the Kaaba, Zurich was the geographic fortuity, a moment in time and place, for what is in fact a timeless journey.

Another person who has reported such a worldwide pilgrimage and who also wound up and remains in Zurich, is colleague and friend John Hill—an Irishman of no country, a pilgrim of the soul. In his comprehensive book exploring the archetype of home, *At Home in the*

World, he recounts his peregrinations and reaches some important conclusions about homecoming. John concludes something similar to what I did. As he finishes his long manuscript, wondering if his preoccupation with "home" is a form of regression, he dreams of his childhood home, replete with luminous stones. When he shortly after walks on a beach in Patmos, Greece, and sees similar stones, he realizes that his "home" was not back in Eire but, after his long journey, "*the house was my book on home.*"[1] Home is transformed from place into process, from physical locus to spiritual locomotion.

I have discovered that there is no home to which we may return "out there," no Valhalla to attain; there is only *the journey*. Today, I understand what I could not as a child: *The journey is our home. Our home is our journey.* By this I mean there is no place to arrive where we know it all, where we are finally content. Inside each of us, there is a hunger, a burning desire to know, to explore. Why, after all, did the bear climb over the mountain, as the song has it? "To see what he could see." As Jung pointed out once, this quickening of the spirit in each of us helps us overcome what he took as our greatest temptation: torpor, sloth, a resting on the oars.

Speaking of oars, I have on my office printer a quote from *The Odyssey*:

> I will stay with it and endure.
> And if the heaving sea has shaken my raft to pieces
> then I will swim.

Why do you think I have that quote there? To remind me to swim, to keep moving forward into whatever curiosity, whatever mystery beckons. There are many who seek peace and contentment and a tranquility above the fray. I, too, am tempted by this possibility, but I have come to conclude that our journey is found in moving onward, setting forth anew before we grow complacent, self-satisfied, and spiritually inert. Even if we arrive "home," telluric forces, whether inner, social, or epochal, will agitate to pry us out of that place. If our home is our journey, then growth, flow, and development will become familiar companions.

Many of you will know and love that poem by C. P. Cavafy titled "Ithaka," the home port of Odysseus. Imagining that Odysseus, weary with ten years of slaughter and tumult on the plains of Troy and another ten years of sea wrack and blood spume on the wine-dark sea, would welcome a bit of a rest at his home in Ithaka, might wish to pull up a lawn chair, open a six pack, and watch the ball game, or something like that. Instead, he whispers in this traveler's ear:

> Ithaka gave you the marvelous journey.
> Without her you wouldn't have set out.
> She has nothing left to give you now.
>
> And if you find her poor, Ithaka won't have fooled you.
> Wise as you will have become, so full of experience,
> you'll have understood by then what these Ithakas mean.[2]

And so we learn: our various Ithakas give us our journey; our journey is our home. All arrivals are way stations on the path to the next journey; if not that, they are the tombstones of a dead soul.

And so, in a conclusion perhaps disappointing to the reader, we find that we will *always* live in in-between times, between what has been reached and exhausted and what approaches over the curve of the horizon. We best live through times of change, loss, challenge when we live this journey as fully as we can, engaging both the sirens with their seductive distractions and the sea serpents with their intimidations as they rise from the spindrift of our lives; guided by our natural curiosity and longing, perhaps we may drop our plumb line into those same guiding currents that ran through the souls of the ancients and that run through ours. Why should we think, on the one hand, that our life should be any easier than theirs was? Or why should we think, on the other hand, that we are not equipped by the gods with the same resources they had to find within themselves? Why should we think that their journey obviates ours? Why should we think we are exempt from casting off from the familiar shore? Kierkegaard reminds us that merchant vessels hug the shore, but blue-water mariners open their orders on the high seas.

Are we afraid? Of course. Remember only psychotics and the deluded are not. But since when is that an excuse for not showing up in life?

Do you feel alone? Yes, we all have this journey to make, this passage compelled by the opaque gods to all of us during times in-between. Only you can take your journey; only your map is right for you. Others have to find their way. But you must know there are many others on the same voyage, with similar wreckage behind as well, facing similar fears, and riddled with similar self-doubt. And still, the open sea, the realm of the imaginally limitless beckons. All we can do is show up, grab an oar, do the best we can, and, while alone, sail this same sibilant sea together. After we take up that oar, no matter the outcome, we can say with that other voyager, Aeneas, "I have lived; I have finished the course Fortune assigned me."[3]

NOTES

CHAPTER 1

1. Arnold, "The Buried Life."
2. Rilke, *Letters to a Young Poet*, letter VIII.
3. Ibid.
4. Nietzsche, *The Joyful Science.*
5. Yeats, "Nineteen Hundred and Nineteen," lines 25–26.
6. Jung, *CW 13: Alchemical Studies*, para. 54.
7. MacLeish, "Hypocrite Auteur."

CHAPTER 2

1. Solzhenitsyn, *The Red Wheel*, node 3, book 1.
2. Beckett, *Waiting for Godot.*
3. Shakespeare, *Macbeth*, act IV, scene 2, lines 75–77.
4. Harari, *Homo Deus*, 200–201.
5. See Ray Kurzweil's *The Singularity Is Near* for further details. As one wag put it, the singularity is "the Rapture for nerds."
6. Jung, *CW 18: The Symbolic Life*, para. 627.
7. Tillich, "The Lost Dimension in Religion."

CHAPTER 3

1. Carl Jung, CW 7. *Two Essays on Analytic Psychology*. Para. 409.

CHAPTER 4

1. Shakespeare, *Hamlet*, act III, scene I, lines 61–62.

2. Marion Woodman, Lecture at Jung Center of Houston, Texas.

3. Milton, *Paradise Lost*, book 4, line 73.

4. *Suppression* is a conscious, deliberate act to avoid the pressing issue. *Repression* is an unconscious, reflexive relocation of the threat into the unconscious in order to avoid its painful encounter. *Dissociation* is an involuntary shift of present identification to an alternative, safer reality or construct in order to protect the threatened ego consciousness.

5. Among these personality disorders are *avoidance* (Avoidant Personality Disorder, Schizoid Personality Disorder, Dissociative Personality Disorder); *compliance* (Dependent Personality Disorder); and *power* (Antisocial Personality Disorder, Obsessive-Compulsive Personality Disorder).

6. These disorders arise out of an insufficiently reassuring and emotionally deficit environment and make their appearances as disorders of *self-image* (Paranoid Personality Disorder); inordinate *neediness* (Borderline Personality Disorder); and *power mechanisms* (Narcissistic Personality Disorder, Histrionic Personality Disorder).

7. Jung, *The Zofingia Lectures*, 73.

CHAPTER 5

1. Eliot, "Baudelaire," in *Selected Essays*, 429.

2. Jung, *CW 11: Psychology and Religion: West and East*, para. 36.

3. All quotes in this section are from Sophocles' *Antigone*, unless otherwise noted.

4. All quotes in this section are from Shakespeare's *Hamlet*, unless otherwise noted.

5. All quotes in this section are from Eliot's "The Love Song of J. Alfred Prufrock," unless otherwise noted.

6. *Good Housekeeping*, December 1961.

CHAPTER 6

1. Arnold, "The Buried Life."

CHAPTER 8

1. One of these worthies recently informed his flock that "God" had told him that his servant should be equipped with a new jet plane to visit his brethren scattered around the world. One would not expect a special vessel of divine revelation, as he was, to ride in the cheap seats of commercial airlines, not to mention having to pass through the TSA checkpoint. Naturally, this latest channel of divine will need to be funded by the faithful themselves.

2. Battiste, "Police Raid 'Secret Archives' of Houston Archdiocese."

3. In the 1860s, Dickinson wrote in a letter to critic Thomas Wentworth Higginson, "The sailor cannot see the North, but he knows the needle can," suggesting that all of us need to know we have a compass and to risk reliance on it.

4. Robert Johnson's *Inner Work: Using Dreams and Active Imagination for Personal Growth* and James Hall's *Jungian Dream Interpretation* are two introductory books that can help you enter the dream field with more understanding.

5. Dunn, "Loves," *Landscape at the End of the Century*, 94.

6. Rilke, *Letters to a Young Poet*, letter 7.

CHAPTER 9

1. Jung, *CW 13: Alchemical Studies*, 15.

2. Ibid., 18.

3. Moustakas, *Loneliness*, ix.

4. Jung, *CW 13: Psychology and Alchemy*, para. 32.

5. Jung, *Memories, Dreams, Responsibilities*, 356.

6. Jung, *The Archetypes and the Collective Unconscious*, 253. If you think Jung an alarmist in his time, think how the world now runs the risk of imminent disaster through the proliferation of the nuclear powers and how we continue our profligate habits in the face of global warming. We can't argue that we don't know better. And shame on those who deliberately led us astray in service to profits and political expediency!

7. Ibid.

8. Dunn, "The Good News," in *Here and Now Poems*.

9. Jung, *CW 11: Psychology and Religion: West and East*, para. 140.

10. Jung, *CW 8: The Structure and Dynamics of the Psyche*, para. 786.

11. When I look at my life archetypally, I see it has been in service, metaphorically, to the god Hermes. Hermes/Mercurius not only facilitates communication among the primal powers but also is a god of *in-betweens*—in between the transcendent realm and the cares of earthly life, in between gods and peoples, and in between the ego world and the vast mystery of the psyche. While serving as a servant "priest" of Hermes may not be recognized by the tax authorities or government statisticians, it has been a most meaningful, if unexpected, vocation.

12. Jung, *CW 8: The Structure and Dynamics of the Psyche*, para. 815.

13. All quotes in this section are from Jung's *Symbols of Transformation*, unless otherwise noted.

14. Jung, *CW 14: Mysterium Coniunctionis*, para. 778.

15. Sartre, cited in Bakewell, *At the Existentialists Café*, 10.

16. Jung, *CW 13: Psychology and Alchemy*, para. 32.

17. All quotes from here to the end of this section are from Jung, *CW 16: The Practice of Psychotherapy*, para. 82.

18. Jung, *Memories, Dreams, Reflections*, 287.

19. *Dasein*, the German word for "existence," is "being here." And we are "thrown here," as Martin Heidegger added.

20. I am quite aware that in speaking of the essential mystery of being, I turned to a noun (the "Thing"), implying its objective presence; however, I am of course speaking metaphorically and remind us always that the elusive "Thing" is never the "Thing." That would make it a noun, an object, observable by our various telemetries. But all that is a trap of our grammar. To speak of "anything" is to make it a "thing," when it may not be a thing at all. As Kierkegaard said, "The God that can be named is not God." Or the Eastern version, "The Tao that can be named is not the Tao."

AFTERWORD

1. Hill, *At Home in the World*, 261.

2. Cavafy, "Ithaka."

3. Virgil, *The Aeneid*.

BIBLIOGRAPHY

Arnold, Matthew. "The Buried Life." poets.org/poem/buried-life.

Bakewell, Sarah. *At the Existentialist Café: Freedom, Being, and Apricot Cocktails.* New York: Other Press, 2016.

Battiste, Nikki. "Police Raid 'Secret Archives' of Houston Archdiocese in Sex Abuse Probe." *CBS News*, November 28, 2018. cbsnews.com/news/houston-archdiocese-secret-archives-private-documents-seized-in-sex-abuse-probe/.

Beckett, Samuel. *Waiting for Godot.* New York: Grove Press, 1911.

Camus, Albert. *The Fall.* New York: Vintage Books, 1963.

Cavafy, C. P. "Ithaka." Translated by Edmund Keeley, 1975. poetryfoundation.org/poems/51296/ithaka-56d22eef917ec.

Dunn, Stephen. *Here and Now: Poems.* New York: Norton, 2011.

———. *New and Selected Poems: 1974–1994.* New York: Norton, 1994.

———. *Landscape at the End of the Century.* New York: Norton and Norton, 1991.

Eliot, T. S. "Baudelaire." In *Selected Essays.* New York: Harcourt, Brace, 1932.

———. "The Love Song of J. Alfred Prufrock." In *Prufrock and Other Observations.* New York: A. A. Knopf, 1920.

Hall, James A. *Jungian Dream Interpretation: A Handbook of Theory and Practice.* Toronto: Inner City Books, 1983.

Hill, John. *At Home in the World: Sounds and Symmetries of Belonging.* New Orleans: Spring Journal Books, 2010.

Jung, Carl Gustav. *Collected Works (CW). Twenty Volumes.* Princeton, NJ: Princeton University Press, 1953–79.

———. *The Zofingia Lectures.* Princeton, NJ: Princeton University Press, 1983.

Kurzweil, Ray. *The Singularity Is Near: When Humans Transcend Biology.* New York: Penguin, 2006.

MacLeish, Archibald. "Hypocrite Auteur." In *Collected Poems*. New York: Houghton Mifflin Harcourt, 1952.

Milton, John. *Paradise Lost*. New York: Penguin Classics, 2003.

Moustakas, Clark E. *Loneliness*. New York: Prentice-Hall, 1961.

Nietzsche, Friedrich. *The Gay Science. The Portable Nietzsche*. Edited by Walter Kaufmann. New York: Penguin, 1977.

Rilke, Rainer Maria. *Letters to a Young Poet*. New York: Norton and Norton, 1993.

Seneca, Lucius. *The Stoic Philosophy of Seneca*. Edited by Moses Hadas. New York: W. W. Norton, 1958.

Shakespeare, William. *The Tragedy of Hamlet. Collected Works of Shakespeare*. Edited by David Bevington. New York: Pearson, 2013.

———. *The Tragedy of Macbeth. Collected Works of Shakespeare*. Edited by David Bevington. New York: Pearson, 2013.

Solzhenitsyn, Aleksandr. *The Red Wheel*. South Bend: University of Notre Dame Press, 2019.

Sophocles. *The Complete Plays of Sophocles*. Edited by Robert Bagg. New York: Harper, 2011.

Tillich, Paul. "The Lost Dimension in Religion." *Saturday Evening Post*, June 14, 1958.

Woodman, Marion. *Addiction to Perfection*. Toronto: Inner City Books, 1982.

Yeats, William Butler. "Nineteen Hundred and Nineteen." In *The Tower*. 1928. csun.edu/~hceng029/yeats/yeatspoems/NineteenNinete.

INDEX

abandonment, 41, 51–53, 122–23
  low self-worth and, 51, 148n6
  narcissism and, 52–53, 148n6
  neediness and, 52, 148n6
  overcompensation and, 51
Abraham and Isaac, 104–5
accountability, 84–85, 89–90, 93
  personal, 66, 84–85, 120–21
  summons for, 89–90, 93–94
active imagination, 28–29, 30, 130–31
addictions, 11–12, 42–47
  addictive hook, 43
  addictive pattern, 43–44
  commonality of, 42
  compulsions and, 45–46
  fears and, 44–45
  food, 40, 44
  freedom from, 46–47
  heroic will and, 45
  as rational response to real anxiety, 47
  as reflexive anxiety management systems, 11, 43–47
  reflexive behaviors and, 44–46
  routine and, 43–44
  smoking, 43
  Twelve Step programs, 45, 46
  unbidden ideas and, 44–46
Adler, Alfred, 130
Aeneas, 145
Aeschylus, 70, 71, 80
aesthetic, 104–5
A.I. *See* artificial intelligence (A.I.)
Alcoholics Anonymous (AA), 39, 113
  Jung's letter to Bill W., 46
anger, 11–12, 89
  negative anima and, 99
  righteous violence, 12
  turned within, 50, 89

animus and anima, 98, 99–100
antidepressants, 38
Antigone, 63, 65–72, 81
  authority conflict in, 65, 67–72
  choice, dilemma of, 65–69
  choices, consequences of, 66–67, 69, 70–72
  control, lack of (Fate), 65–66
  Creon in, 67–72, 81
  developmental drive within us (Destiny), 66
  Fate, Destiny, Hubris, and Hamartia in, 66, 71
  nemesis (consequences), 71
  Oedipus, Eteocles, and Polynices, 67
  personal accountability, 66
  right relationship with the gods, 67, 71, 79
  suffering, and humbling of tragic figure, 67
  tragic figure (Creon), 67, 69–72, 79
  tragic flaw (Hamartia), 66, 70–71
  tragic vision of life, 65–66, 71, 79
  witness character (Tiresias), 70
anxiety, 39–42
  addictions and, 11, 43–47
  archaic anxieties, 39–42
  bringing into consciousness, 45
  crises in literature, 63–81
  facing, 40–41
  fears and, 40–41, 46
  functions of, 39–40
  ignoring problems and, 38
  overwhelmment and, 41
  paralyzing anxiety, 40–41
  reflexive anxiety management systems, 11, 43–47
  stuck places and, 39–42
  uncertainty and, 14
  See also unease in life

archaic anxieties, 39–42

archaic interpretations of self and world, 53

archetypes, 33, 117–18, 138
  in *Antigone* and *Hamlet,* 79
  hero/heroine, 118, 131
  as organizing/compensatory energy, 117–18
  transcendent Other, 118

Aristotle, 35

Arnold, Matthew, 2, 93–94

artificial intelligence (A.I.), 16

At Home in the World (Hill), 142–43

attachment, 109, 122–23

attention, 30, 88

authority, 22, 102–3
  choice and, 68–69, 102
  conflicting authorities, 68–70, 133
  developmental drive within us (Destiny), 66
  lack of control (Fate), 65–66
  personal authority, 22, 26–27, 60, 68–69
  personal authority, recovering, 83, 91–92, 102–3
  received authority, 22, 67–72, 102
  received authority in *Antigone,* 67–72
  rulers, divinely appointed, 9–10
  transition of, 22
  See also god(s)

avoidance, 49, 148n4
  ignoring problems, 38
  overwhelmment and, 49
  personality disorders of, 148n5

Basho, 139

Bateson, Gregory, 42

Baudelaire, Charles, 64

Bauer, Jan, 124

Bhagavad Gita, 111

birth/growth/death cycle, 4, 26–27

blame, 126

Bonhoeffer, Dietrich, 69, 105–6, 129

bread and circuses, 13

"The Buried Life" (Arnold), 2, 93–94

Campbell, Joseph, 118

Camus, Albert, 17–18

case histories, fiction of, 34–35

casino adventure of author, 141–42

Cavafy, C. P., 144

change, 1–3, 101–16, 139
  changing times, navigating through, 101–16
  going *through* hard times, 111
  grief/grieving, 109–11
  historic responses to, 16–19
  loss, times of, 109–11
  nature, clues of, 107–8
  self-image and choices, 103–6
  spiritual maturity, 111–16
  steadfastness in, 119, 139
  "What abides amid change?," 139

Chekhov, Anton, 123

choice, 31, 101–6, 133–34
  authority and, 68–69, 102, 133
  consequences of, 66–67, 69, 70–72, 106
  dilemma of, 65–69, 104–6
  factors influencing, 68, 101
  fearsome choices, 104–6
  hubris and, 66, 71
  Jung on, 69, 133–34
  Kant on, 66
  in literature, 33, 65–72
  not enough information for, 66, 108
  predisposition to certain, 66, 68
  Socrates and, 68
  teleological suspension of the ethical, 70, 105
  "the third" in, 69
  unconscious, choice made in, 64
  values and, 67–69
  See also authority

codependence, 50

collective unconscious, 33, 117

compass, 106, 149n3

compensation, 47–53

complex(es), 76
  in *Hamlet,* 44, 72, 76
  "Hamlet complex," 44

compliance, 50, 148n5
  in *Antigone,* 67
compulsions, 45–46
  repetition compulsion, 49, 86
connection
  disconnection, 23–24, 107, 118
  loss of, 11, 12
  need for, 46, 111–12, 122
  technology/internet and, 121–22
conscious mind, 136
control
  controlling behaviors, 52
  fantasy of, 87
  See also authority
cosmic plan, 13
courage, 47, 131
creationism, 14

daimon, 128–30
Dante, 9, 22, 32, 78
data/big data, 15–16
death, 3, 109–11
  birth/growth/death cycle, 4
  evolution through, 3, 4
  grief/grieving, 109–11
  life expectancy, 10
  of old ways/times, 1–2
decisions. *See* choice
"defeated by ever-larger things" (Rilke), 3
defenses, 60
  avoidance, 49
  compliance, 50
  low self-worth, 51
  narcissism, 52–53
  neediness, 52
  power/controlling behaviors, 50–51
  denial, 110
depression, 50, 89
  negative anima and, 99
depth psychology, 21–61
  active imagination, 28–29, 30
  attending our own stories, 24–25
  choice in, 68
  dialogue with self, 24, 27
  dreams in, 25–276, 28–30, 56–59

framing experiences in, 24–25
journals, 27–28, 30
life patterns, reading, 24–25
literature, study of, 30–36
personal stories, examining, 24–25
practices of, 27–30
principles of, 37–61
psyche in, 23–24
relationships, 48–49
symptoms and, 24, 37–38
unconscious in, 23, 33, 39, 44–46
whole person approach, 23
See also depth psychology principles
Depth Psychology and a New Ethic
  (Neumann), 103–4
depth psychology principles,
  I. It's not about what it's about,
    37–47, 113
  II. What you see is compensation for
    what you don't see, 47–53
  III. All is metaphor, 53–61
  abandonment, 41, 51–53
  addictions, 42–47
  archaic anxieties, 39–42
  archaic interpretations, 53
  fears and, 40–41
  getting below what we see, 53
  overwhelmment, 41, 49–51
  pool of anxiety, 38
  stuck places, 38–42
  symptoms, searching for meaning
    from, 37–38, 56
  unconscious and, 39–40, 44–46
destiny, 66, 137
disconnection, 23–24, 107, 118
dissociation, 49, 148n4
distractions, 10–11
  anger, 12
  drugs and alcohol, 11
  food, 11, 40
  news and scandals, 17–18, 102
  panem et circum (bread and
    circuses), 13
  shopping, 10–11, 15, 132
diversions. *See* distractions
Dostoevsky, Fyodor, 5

dreams, 25–26, 28–30, 56–59, 103,
    149n4
  active imagination and, 28–29
  attending to, 57, 103, 107
  healing and, 92
  language of, 56–59, 107, 149n4
  lucid dreaming, 29
  wisdom of, 57–59, 107
Dunn, Stephen, 111, 127

ego, 6, 87, 100, 131, 133–34
  split-off, 111–12
Eliot, George, 4
Eliot, T.S., 64, 77
  The Love Song of J. Alfred Prufrock,
    63–64, 77–80
  The Wasteland, 79
energy, 7, 56, 107, 130–31
  compensatory, 97
  displaced, 7–8
  psyche and, 56
  transformations of, 7
  withdrawal/waning of, 24, 56, 64, 88
evolution, 4

fairy tales, 95
  "The Maiden with No Hands," 95–99
The Fall (Camus), 17–18
fantasies
  education, 12–13
  happiness, 10, 136
  world was better before, 12
fate, 66
Faulkner, William, 25
fear(s), 130–34
  addictions and, 44–45
  anxiety and, 40–41, 46
  bringing into consciousness, 45
  compliance and, 50
  facing, 45, 46, 145
  fearful life, living, 131–32
  going through, 46
  Jung on, 130–34
  Kierkegaard on, 104–5
  paralysis of, 40, 81

Fear and Trembling (Kierkegaard), 104–5

feeling function, 55, 107
feelings, 55, 56
  as messages from psyche, 55
fiction of case histories, 34–35
fight, flight, or freeze (in *Hamlet*), 72–77
food, 40, 44, 111
  diets, 45
framing experiences, 24–25
Freud, Sigmund, 49, 107, 122
fundamentalism, 14–15

gender, 95–100
  animus and anima, 98, 99–100
  the Devil (in "Maiden" tale), 96, 98,
    100
  divided loyalties, 96
  feminine and masculine, valuing
    equally, 97–98, 99–100
  healing of wounds, 96, 98, 99–100
  integration of opposites, 99–100
  "The Maiden with No Hands," 95–99
  miller as trickster, 95–96
  nature (Great Mother) as healer, 96
  negative animus/anima, 99
  the opposite within each gender,
    97–98, 99–100
  patriarchal wounding, 97–98
  sacred marriage (Hieros Gamos), 97,
    100
  wounding of men, 98–99
  wounding of women, 95–98
generalization (overgeneralization), 87
Gilbert, Jack, 21
god(s), 1–8, 14–15, 138
  Apollo, 104
  authority of, 9–10, 68–69, 102
  "the awful grace of God" (Aeschylus),
    70, 71
  belief in invisible, 7
  daimon and, 128–29
  death of, 1–2, 19
  divine/cosmic plan, 13
  divine rulers, 9–10
  "God is dead" (Nietzsche), 4–5, 18
  Imago Dei (god image), 15
  intermediaries for, 102, 128–30

Jung on, 5–6, 7, 80
Jung's definition of God, 80
Machine, Economics, Materialism, and Data, 15–16
neurosis and, 5, 7, 138
other names for, 5–8, 15, 138
the Other and, 6, 111–12, 118
Pan, 1–2
reconnection with, 111–12
revisioning of, 80–81
right relationship with, 67, 71, 79–80
as sources of inspiration, 4
struggle with, and tragic vision of life, 79
surrogates/substitutes for, 2, 8, 15–16, 19, 112
"without God, all things are possible" (Dostoevsky), 5
Zeus, 6
Goethe, 139
Gospel of Thomas, 90
Greene, Graham, 114
grief/grieving, 109–11
growth, 3–4, 92, 112, 129–30
difficult times and, 109, 110, 119

hamartia (tragic flaw), 66, 70–71
Hamlet, 72–77, 81, 137
character of Hamlet, 33, 44, 74
complexes in, 44, 72, 76
as depiction of common/modern issues, 72–73, 76–77
dilemma of Hamlet, 33, 72–73, 81
fractured psyche, 73
ghostly father, 74
Hamlet as his own worst problem, 73, 76–77
"Hamlet complex," 44
in-between state of things, 74–75
reluctance to act, 72–73, 76, 81
stuckness of, 72–73, 76–77, 81
"To be, or not to be," 75
tragedy, or irony?, 73
happiness, xii, 136
choosing meaning over, 84
fantasy of, 10, 136

self-help genre and, 136
Harari, Yuval Noah, 15–16
Hauntings (Hollis), 49
healing, 83–94, 112
accountability and, 89–90
aspirations, recovering, 92
critical assignments in, 83–84
dreams and, 28, 92
of gendered wounds, 98, 99–100
as homecoming, 141
integration of opposites, 99–100
meaning and, 84
nature equips us for, 85
permission, recovery of, 90–91
personal authority, recovering, 83, 91–92
principles for, 85–93
psychopathology, gift of, 87–88
returning to ourselves, 2, 85, 111–12
sense of purpose, 84–85
serving what wants to enter the world through us, 92–93
spirituality and, 83–84
splits within, healing, 92–93, 99–100
stories and, 85–87
healthy neurotics, 51
helicopter parents, 123
Hell, 46, 81
Dante's, 78
Prufrock's, 78
Satan and, 46
hero/heroine, 118, 131
The Hero with a Thousand Faces (Campbell), 118
heroic will, 45
Hieros Gamos (sacred marriage), 97, 100
Hill, John, 142–43
history
personal, 30–31
relational, 50
Hölderlin, Friedrich, 130
holy marriage (Hieros Gamos), 97, 100
homecoming, 139, 141–45
the journey as home, 143–44

Where is your home?, 142–43

"Homecoming" (Hölderlin), 130

Homo Deus: A Brief History of Tomorrow (Harari), 15

hubris, 66, 71, 79, 104

ideas, 44
  unbidden, 44–46

illness. *See* healing

images
  metaphor and, 54
  storehouse of (in literature), 32–33

imagination, 85–86
  active imagination, 28–29, 30, 130–31
  literature and, 35

in-between state, 9–20, 144
  change, responses to, 16–19, 101–16
  deaths and endings, 3, 9, 10, 109–11
  description of, 2–3, 9–20
  Hamlet and, 74–75
  in literature, 63–81
  living in, 19–20, 101–16, 144
  passages and, 3
  Prufrock and, 77–78
  underlying causes of, 2–3
  unease in life, 2, 3–4, 11, 84

inflation (hubris), 66, 71, 79

insights, 28, 47

inspiration, 4

instinct, 2, 41, 83, 98

internet, 121–22

invisible, belief in, 7

"Ithaka" (Cavafy), 144

Ixion, 46

Jesus of Nazareth, 106

journals/journaling, 27–28, 30

journey, as home, 143–45

Jung, Carl, 16–17, 117–39
  animus and anima, 99–100
  archetypes, 117–18
  on choice, 69, 133–34
  collective unconscious, 33, 117
  on communication from presence

within, 60, 128–30
  cultural context of, 17
  cure for loneliness is solitude, 121–25
  definition of God, 80
  family of origin, personal feelings on, 16–17
  fear and lethargy as opponents, 130–34, 143
  on god(s), 5–6, 9, 80
  on meaning/conduct of life, 136–39, 141
  Memories, Dreams, Reflections (memoir), 137–38
  on neuroses, 5–6, 7, 65, 97, 129, 138
  observations on meaning, 117–39
  opposites, tension of, 59, 114
  on the psyche, 31–32, 128–30
  on psychotherapy, 134–35, 136
  real issues of life not solvable, 119–21
  Shadow, The, 126–27
  shadows, addressing, 125–27
  "something bigger than ourselves," 17, 18
  Symbols of Transformation, 130–31
  on technology, 125–26
  on transformation, 1
  on unease, 9
  we are the meaning-makers, 134–36

Kant, Immanuel, 51, 66

Kennedy, Robert F., 71

Kierkegaard, Søren, 70, 89–90, 104–5, 144
  Fear and Trembling, 104–5
  teleological suspension of the ethical, 70, 105

King, Martin Luther, Jr., 69, 71, 129

knowing/knowledge
  feeling function and, 55, 107
  internal source for, 60, 102–3, 134–35
  knowing what's right, 56, 65, 69, 72, 83, 84, 92, 107–8, 135–36
  locus of knowing, 17, 20, 57
  not-knowing, 112
  primal, 60, 83

learned helplessness, 50, 89

lethargy, 130–34, 143

Letter to the Romans (St. Paul), 72–73

Letters to a Young Poet (Rilke), 3–4, 85, 90, 113–14

life
  facing our obstacles, 132
  life patterns, 24–25, 50–53
  meaning in/meaning of, 136–39, 141
  purpose in, 10, 84–85
  real issues not solvable, but may be outgrown, 119–21
  of service, 84–85, 90, 92–94, 132–34
  "Shut up. Suit up. Show up." mantra for, 132
  symbolic life, 138

life expectancy, 10

light, as energy, 7

literature, 30–36, 63–81
  archetypes in, 33, 79
  choice, nature of, 33, 65–72
  "fiction of case histories," 34–35
  human condition and, 34, 81
  images, storehouse of, 32–33
  imagination, broadening of, 35
  metaphor and, 32
  as preparation for engaging the soul (psyche), 32–35
  reasons for study of, 32–35, 81

literature case studies, 63–81
  Antigone, 63, 65–72
  Hamlet, 63, 72–77
  Prufrock, 63–64, 77–80
  Fate, Destiny, Hubris, and Hamartia, 66, 71
  in-between state depicted, 74–75, 77–78, 81
  Oedipus, 67, 70, 80
  resilience and, 63, 81
  revisioning of the gods, 80–81
  right relationship with the gods, 67, 71, 79–80
  stuckness of Hamlet, 72–73, 76–77
  tragic figure, suffering and humbling of, 67, 70–72, 80
  tragic flaw, 66, 71

tragic vision of life, 65–66, 71, 79–80
  See also Antigone; Hamlet; Prufrock

Living an Examined Life (Hollis), 83, 90

locus of knowing, 17, 20, 57

loneliness, 121–25
  fear of, 18, 122
  as "highest and most decisive experience," 124
  loss and abandonment, 122–23
  marriage and, 123

"Loneliness" (Rilke), 123

longing of the soul, 11

loss, 109–11

"The Lost Dimension in Religion" (Tillich), 18–19

"Loves" (Dunn), 111

The Love Song of J. Alfred Prufrock. See Prufrock

Machine, 15

MacLeish, Archibald, 8

Magritte, 34

"The Maiden with No Hands," 95–99
  See also gender

Mandela, Nelson, 129

maps
  disappearance of old maps, xi, 1–8
  roadmap to life's journey, 3, 22, 134

Markham, Edwin, 1

marriage, holy (Hieros Gamos), 97

Marsyras, flaying of, 104

materialism, 15

meaning, 10, 19, 24, 84, 108, 117–39
  addressing our shadows, 125–27
  cure for loneliness is solitude, 121–25
  disconnection from, 118
  fear and lethargy as opponents, 130–34, 143
  found in whole picture, 110–11
  as goal of life, 24
  Jung's observations on, 117–39
  psyche wants to be heard, 128–30
  real issues of life not solvable, 119–21
  suffering and, 113–14

we are the meaning-makers, 134–36
where from and whither to?, 136–39
Memories, Dreams, Reflections (Jung),
  137–38
men, wounding of, 98–99
  See also gender
metaphor, 53–61, 130–31
  death of, 8
  dreams and, 56–59, 107
  energy and, 56
  feelings and, 55, 56
  meaning of word, 54
  moments of meaning and, 56
  trusting the messages, 55–61
  using literature to understand, 32
Moustakas, Clark, 123
muse, 129
mystery, 21, 80, 107, 112
  of being, 139, 151n20
  dialogue with, 23
  participation in, 138
myth(s), 6, 20
  fundamentalism and scientism,
    13–16
  Ixion, 46

"Naming Storms" (Hollis, Tim), 115
narcissism, 52–53, 148n6
nature, 4, 85, 107–8
  alignment with, 79–80, 92–93, 128
  birth/growth/death cycle, 4, 26–27
  dynamics of, 4
  evolution through death, 2
  humans as equipped by nature, 30,
    85, 110, 116, 135
  survival, 110
  vital clues to, 107–8
neediness, 52, 148n6
nemesis (consequences), 71
Neumann, Erich, 103–4
neurosis, 15
  causes of, 47
  healthy neurotics, 51
  Jung on, 5–6, 7, 65, 97, 129, 138
  necessity of risk to cure, 65

as neglected or repressed God, 5, 7, 138
as price of civilization (Freud), 107
split within/one-sidedness, 47, 51, 97
New Year's resolutions, 44
Nietzsche, Friedrich
  "God is dead," 4–5, 18
  humans as "the sick animal," 2
nightmares, 5
nights, dark, 3–4
nostalgia, 8, 12
"Not my will but Thine," 106
numinous, the, 17, 113, 116, 119, 133

obsessions, 45–46
Odyssey, 143–44
Oedipus, 67, 70, 80, 106
opposites
  gender and, 97–98, 99–100
  integration of, 99–100
  tension of, 59, 114
Other, 6, 18, 111–12, 118
  attachment to, 124–25
  relationship through symbols and
    metaphor, 54–55, 59–60
  Wholly Other, 6
overgeneralization, 87
overwhelmment, 41, 49–51
  avoidance and, 49, 148n4
  compliance and, 50
  power dynamics and, 50–51, 148n6

Paradise Lost, 46
Pascal, Blaise, 11
past
  framing experiences from, 24–25
  as not dead (Faulkner), 25
patriarchal wounding, 97–98
patterns, 2–3, 50–53, 68, 86, 118
  behavioral patterns, 23, 33
  emergence, fruition, decay, and
    decline, 4
  past and, 24–25
  "reading" of, 25
  symptoms and, 24

Paul's *Letter to the Romans,* 72–73

permission, recovery of, 90–91

persistence, 47

personal authority, 22, 26–27, 60
  in *Antigone,* 68–69
  recovering, 83, 91–92, 102–3

personality disorders, 51, 52, 148nn5-6

phenomenology, 6–7

Picasso, 34

The Power and the Glory (Greene), 114

power dynamics, 50–51, 91
  personality disorders and, 148n5, 148n6

powerlessness, 16, 89, 91

learned helplessness, 50, 89

Primary Phenomenon, 6

problems
  being stuck, 38–42
  ignoring, 38

procrastination, 38

progress, trade-offs of, 12

Prufrock (*The Love Song of J. Alfred Prufrock*), 63–64, 77–80
  alignment with nature and the gods, 79–80
  heroic aspirations, 78, 79
  hundred indecisions in, 78
  in-between state, 77–78, 81
  suffering and, 79, 80

psyche, 17, 23–24, 128–30
  attending to, 17, 30, 59–60
  communication from, 53–61, 88, 92–93, 128–30
  as compensatory, 48
  daimon, 128–30
  dreams and, 28–30
  energy systems and, 56, 88
  expression of, 128–30
  feelings and, 55
  growth of, 130
  healing of gender wounds, 100
  journaling and, 27–28, 30
  knowing, Jung on, 31–32
  literature and, 32–35
  metaphors, communication through, 53–61

psychopathology and, 24
  as self-regulating system, 47–48
  sense of rightness from, 56, 92, 107–8
  symbols, communication through, 54–55, 59–60
  trusting messages from, 55–61, 92–93, 102–3

psychology, 21–36
  depth psychology, 21–36
  development of, 21–22
  psyche and, 23–24
  reflection therapy, 87
  See also depth psychology

psychopathology, 24, 87–90
  call to accountability, 89–90
  gift of, 87–88
  psyche and, 24
  as suffering of the soul, 24, 88

psychotherapy
  aim of, 136
  Jung on, 134–35, 136
  as listening to the soul, 93

purpose in life, 10, 84–85
  meaning and, 136–39, 141

questions
  How can we continue to live in a time such as ours?, 19
  How do I live in the world?, 25, 136
  To be, or not to be? (*Hamlet*), 75
  What abides amid change?, 139
  What am I waiting for?, 92
  What are my dreams trying to tell me?, 29–30
  What do my symptoms mean?, 24, 56
  What do we do now that we are happy?, 10–11
  What is deepest within?, 22–24
  What is our calling in times in-between?, 19–20
  What is replacing the old order, old gods?, 10
  What is the meaning of life?, 19, 24, 136
  What wants to enter the world through me?, 91, 92–93
  Where is your home?, 142–43
  Who am I?, 25

rationality, 6
reading
  "reading" our life patterns, 24–25
  "reading" the world, 25, 48
  See also literature
reflection therapy, 87
reflexive anxiety management systems,
    11, 43–47
reflexive behaviors, 44–46
relationships, 48–53
  avoidance and, 49
  compliance and, 50
  engaging with otherness through, 121
  helicopter parents, 123
  power dynamics in, 50–51, 148n6
  repetition in relational dynamics, 49
  solitude and, 123, 125
religion, 6–7, 14–15, 102, 111–12
  creationism, 14
  fundamentalism, 14–15
  "The Lost Dimension in Religion"
    (Tillich), 18–19
  Nietzsche on, 4, 18
  See also god(s)
repetition compulsion, 49, 86
repression, 49, 148n4
resilience, 17, 63, 85, 110–11
resonance, 112–13
responsibility. See accountability
rightness/knowing what's right, 56, 65,
    69, 72, 83, 84, 92, 107–8, 135–36
Rilke, Rainer Maria, 3–4, 85, 90,
    113–14
  answers within yourself, 101
  defeated by ever-larger things, 3
  on healthy relationship, 125
  Letters to a Young Poet, 3–4, 85, 90,
    113–14
  "Loneliness," 123
risk, 65, 131
routine, 43–44

sacred marriage (Hieros Gamos), 97, 100
Sartre, Jean-Paul, 134
Satan, 46, 48

scandals, 17–18, 102
scientism, 13–14
Self/deep Self, 103–6
  See also psyche
self-governance, 25–27
self-image, 103–6, 148n6
self interest, 104–5
self-worth, 41–42, 51, 148n6
Shadow, The, 126–27
shadows, addressing, 125–27
Shakespeare, 63, 72
  Hamlet, 63, 72–77
shopping, 10–11, 15, 132
"Shut up. Suit up. Show up.," 132
Singularity, the, 16
slavery, 91
smoking, 43
social contract, 19, 68
Socrates, 68, 117, 128–29
solitude, 121–25, 134, 145
Solzhenitsyn, Aleksandr, 10
Sophocles, 63, 65
  Antigone, 63, 65–72
The Sorrow Tree, 110
soul, 23–24
  desire for expression, 92–94
  disconnection from, 23–24
  longing of the, 11
  psyche, 17, 23–24
  suffering of (psychopathology), 24, 88
  See also psyche
spirituality, 83–84, 111–16
  growth and, 84, 112
  mystery and, 83–84, 112
  spiritual maturity, 111–16
  spiritual thirst, 2, 46, 93–94
splits within, 107–8, 111–12
  healing, 92–93, 111–12
  neurosis as, 47, 51
  split from nature/internal cues, 2,
    107–8
State, the, 10
steadfastness, 119, 136, 139

stories, 24–25, 49, 85–86
   creating, 85–86
   emotionally charged, 25
   healing and, 85–87
   personal, examining and rewriting, 24–25
   servants and prisoners of, 86–87
stuck places/stuckness, 38–42, 64–65
   abandonment and, 41
   archaic anxieties and, 39–42
   costs of perpetuating, 42
   fears and, 40–41
   first step in letting go of, 47
   Hamlet and, 72–73, 76–77
   overwhelmment and, 41, 42, 50
   perpetuating, 39, 41, 65
   reasons for, 41
   "This isn't working, but I do it very well," 39
suffering
   active vs. passive, 80
   meaning/growth and, 113–14, 119
   of the soul, 24, 88
   thoughtful suffering, 104
   of tragic figure (in literature), 67, 70–72, 80
   tragic suffering, 67, 70–72, 80
suppression, 49, 148n4
Swamplands of the Soul (Hollis), 120–21
symbols, 54–55, 59–60, 107, 130–31
   "symbolic life," 138
   See also metaphor
Symbols of Transformation (Jung), 130–31
symptoms, 37–38, 56, 135
   meaning of, 24, 37–38, 56
   as natural expression of the psyche, 24, 56
   withdrawal/waning of energy as, 24, 56, 64

technology, 121–22
   Jung's critique of, 125–26
Terence, 126
"Thing," 139, 151n20
"the third," 69, 114

thirst, spiritual, 2, 46, 93–94
through (only way through dilemmas is *through*), 3, 39–40, 46, 69, 111
Tillich, Paul, 18–19
Tracking the Gods: The Place of Myth in Modern Life (Hollis), 6
tragic figure, 67, 69–72, 79
tragic flaw, 66, 70–71
tragic suffering, 67, 70–72, 80
tragic vision of life, 65–66, 71, 79–80
treatment plan
   for addictions, 45–47
   diversions, food, addictions as, 11, 18–19
   failing, 8, 11, 14–15, 19, 38, 46
   identification with, 47
   responses to cultural malaise (uneasiness), 8, 11, 14–15, 18–19
   as "what we see," 48

unbidden ideas, 44–46
unconscious, 23, 39
   collective unconscious, 33, 117
   consequences from, 39–40
   decisions made by, 64
   in depth psychology, 23
   engaging with, 23
   symptoms and, 39–42
   unbidden ideas and, 44–46
unconsciousness, seduction of, 131–32
unease in life, 2, 3–4, 84
   current day culture and, 8
   displaced energies and, 7
   Jung on, 9
   loss of felt connection, 11
   Pascal on, 11
   responses to/treatment plan for, 8, 11, 14–15, 18–19
   See also in-between state
unworthiness, 41

values, 8, 126
   choices and, 105–6
vocation, 93

Waiting for Godot (Beckett), 10

The Wasteland (Eliot), 79

Wholly Other, 6

willpower, 45
  heroic will, 45

wisdom. *See* knowing/knowledge

women, wounding of, 95–98
  See also gender

Woodman, Marion, 27, 46

worthiness, 41, 51

wounds
  healing of wounds, 96, 98, 99–100
  patriarchal wounding, 97–98
  separation from natural drives/
    instincts, 2
  wounding of men, 98–99
  wounding of women, 95–98

Yeats, William Butler, 5

ABOUT THE AUTHOR

James Hollis, PhD is a Zurich-trained Jungian analyst, has been a professor of humanities and psychology in various universities, has authored sixteen books, and has spoken on four continents. Additionally, he was a co-founder of the Jung Institute of Philadelphia, and served as Director of the Jung Center of Houston and the Washington Jung Society. Currently, he remains in private practice in Washington, DC, where he lives with his wife Jill, a retired therapist and artist. Together, they have three living children and eight grandchildren.

ABOUT SOUNDS TRUE

Sounds True is a multimedia publisher whose mission is to inspire and support personal transformation and spiritual awakening. Founded in 1985 and located in Boulder, Colorado, we work with many of the leading spiritual teachers, thinkers, healers, and visionary artists of our time. We strive with every title to preserve the essential "living wisdom" of the author or artist. It is our goal to create products that not only provide information to a reader or listener but also embody the quality of a wisdom transmission.

For those seeking genuine transformation, Sounds True is your trusted partner. At SoundsTrue.com you will find a wealth of free resources to support your journey, including exclusive weekly audio interviews, free downloads, interactive learning tools, and other special savings on all our titles.

To learn more, please visit SoundsTrue.com/freegifts or call us toll-free at 800.333.9185.

sounds true
WAKING UP THE WORLD